Walking with the Famous... and the Infamous

by
Roger Seedhouse

Meridian Books

Published 2002 by Meridian Books

ISBN 1-869922-46-8

A catalogue record for this book is available from the British Library

Cover painting by Anne Greatbatch

Character drawings by Yvonne Dunnington

Meridian Books

40 Hadzor Road, Oldbury, West Midlands B68 9LA

Printed in Great Britain by MFP Design & Print, Manchester

Contents

Introduction

There is no doubt that walking is one of our most popular pastimes, and will become increasingly so as people acquire more leisure time. Many books are available to satisfy those who prefer to have their routes prepared for them or like to adopt a theme such as pub walks or canal walks.

It is not easy now to think of something new or a little different from the wealth of trail books available, excellent though most of them are.

I decided that the theme for my next book would be famous historical characters who either lived in Shropshire or who had strong associations with it. Could I indeed write a book of walks around the haunts of these people – where they lived, died or worked – whilst at the same time relating the principal events in their lives? A little research soon revealed there was plenty of material to work on but what really convinced me to do it was my friend's almost throwaway suggestion 'why don't you write it through the eyes of the character concerned, as if they were telling their own story'. Great! I thought, that would be different although it may be crossing the boundary into the literary world a little.

So here is the result and I hope it brings you pleasure as well as an insight into some of the County's more prominent individuals. Whilst I have endeavoured to give a flavour of how those individuals may have spoken or related their tale you must forgive a certain amount of artistic licence. There would not be much point in my writing in the fourteenth century style (even if I could) if you did not understand any of it!

Using this book

The entire narrative is written as though through the eyes of the individual concerned and arranged with normal text, comprising largely of directions, and of paragraphs in italics that are purely life story elements. The latter have been positioned to coincide as much as possible with sections of the walk where they can be read without interruption by too many directional instructions (e.g. along lanes or tracks). It is, therefore, suggested that you read ahead a little further than you might in a normal guide book in order to obtain best advantage in this. For example, if a directional text paragraph ends in something like 'turn left off the lane down an embankment onto the canal towpath' and is followed by several paragraphs in italics you know that there should be ample time to read them before having to worry about the next direction – but a quick look ahead to that direction would be prudent.

Points to consider

1. Wear sensible gear. A good pair of boots is essential; so are waterproofs and warm clothing in less clement weather or when undertaking wild hill walks.

2. If you can, take a map of the area. Landranger (1:50,000 or 1¼ inches to the mile) is the most commonly used but Explorer or the older Pathfinder (both 1:25,000 or 2½ inches to the mile) with much more detail are better. I am not suggesting this because you are likely to get lost but merely as a prudent precaution just in case you do stray off the route or if, perhaps because of deteriorating weather, you want to cut short the walk. A compass is also a valuable item for the same reasons.

3. Some paths, particularly those less well used, can get overgrown in summer. A walking stick can make life a lot easier in such situations and, sometimes, a pair of secateurs. A small first aid kit should also be carried in the event of a close encounter with a bramble or other mishap.

4. The countryside is constantly changing. Seasonal changes can make things which appear obvious or easy to recognise in summer less so in winter and vice-versa. Be wary also of physical changes. The position or type of gate/fence/stile may be altered, field boundaries are changed or even removed altogether, tracks can be diverted (officially or otherwise), etc.

5. A Right of Way is precisely what it says – you have the right to walk along it at all times unimpeded. Fortunately, most County Councils pursue a continuing programme of clearing and waymarking paths, but this is a huge task and many remain obscure. Likewise, most landowners adopt an enlightened attitude towards walkers but occasionally obstructions will be encountered, paths will have been obliterated or diverted or not reinstated after planting has taken place. Try not to be daunted by such things and remember that you have a legal right to pass. Needless to say, common sense should come to the fore in such situations; for example, it may be necessary to take a path around the edge of a cropped field rather than across it or follow an unofficial diversion rather than stick to the line on the map. Any serious obstructions should, however, be reported to Shropshire Council's Rights of Way department.

6. Some animals can create consternation for the walker. Farm dogs are frequently encountered but mostly make a lot of noise rather than cause any physical injury. Again, a walking stick is useful just to be on the safe side. A field of frisky young bullocks is best avoided. Even though they are merely curious or think you have come to feed them, I prefer to skirt around them where possible. Sheep are no problem!

7. Not many pub landlords like muddy boots trampling over their floors. Try to be considerate and, if you cannot clean them off, take them off and leave outside or in a lobby.

8. Last, but not least, REMEMBER THE COUNTRY CODE!

Public transport services to some areas are very limited or even non-existent. Some appropriate telephone numbers are:

British Rail: 0345 484950
Travelline: (Buses and Coaches) 0870 608 2608

About the Author

Roger Seedhouse is a Chartered Surveyor and a partner in a firm of property consultants in the West Midlands. He has lived on the border of Shropshire and Staffordshire all his life and has an extensive knowledge of the Midlands counties. When not ministering to the requirements of his two daughters his spare time is taken up with writing and walking.

He is the author of *Walks to Wet your Whistle, More Walks to Wet your Whistle* and *Walks Through History in the Heart of England*. Visit his website *www.bestwalks.com* for more information.

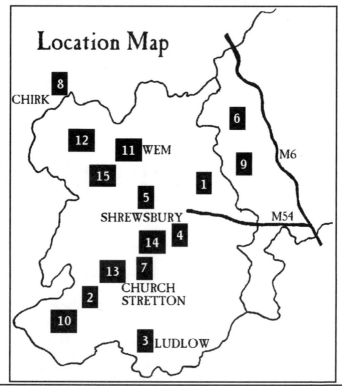

Publishers' Note

Every care has been taken in the preparation of this book. All walks have been independently checked and are believed to be correct at the time of publication. However, no guarantee can be given that they contain no errors or omissions and neither the author nor the publishers can accept any responsibility for loss, damage or inconvenience resulting from the use of this book.

Please remember that the countryside is continually changing: hedges and fences may be remove or re-sited; footbridges and river banks may suffer flood damage; footpaths may be re-routed or ploughed over and not reinstated (as the law requires); concessionary paths may be closed. If you do encounter any such problems please let the publishers know, and please report any obstructions to rights of way to the local authority.

The Famous

1

The Clive of India Trilogy - 1

1725 - 1774

Maps: Landranger 127; Explorer 243
Start: The village of Moreton Say, 3 miles west of Market Drayton. GR 630345
Park: By St. Margaret's Church except when services are in progress or due. Otherwise there are parking facilities at the village hall nearby.
Walk Distance: 3¾ miles
Terrain: Very easy by most standards although some sections can get a little muddy.
Refreshments: None *en route*; the nearest available in Market Drayton.
Associated places of interest: (see Town Map on page 14)
1. The Clive & Coffyne Public House in Market Drayton which contains Clive memorabilia and serves the now famous Clive Pies – see footnote to walk 3. The pub was re-named in 1990 as a dedication to Lord Clive and the Pies. 'Coffyne' actually means 'pie-case' in early English. Open every day from 10.30 a.m. except for Sundays when opening is not until 3 p.m.
2. Market Drayton Grammar school – located to the rear of the church. Now private property but there is a plaque on the front wall.
3. Market Drayton church (St. Mary's). Access to the interior available daily between 11 a.m. – 2 p.m. in summer, 12 noon – 2 p.m. in winter.

They say I'm a hero. Well, if that is the accolade posterity wishes to bestow upon me, then so be it. I'll own that I played no small part in laying the foundation of our once great British Empire in India and was generally regarded as a brilliant soldier. Mark you, if my childhood proffered any indication of future fortunes I was not destined for anything but abject failure.

Life began here in Moreton Say on 29th September 1725; the place of my birth being Styche Hall, then a crumbling Tudor manor house which was replaced in 1762 by the present structure (at my expense!). You will see this from a distance later. The church of St. Margaret is, so to speak, my beginning and my end for I was both baptised and laid to rest here. As regards the latter

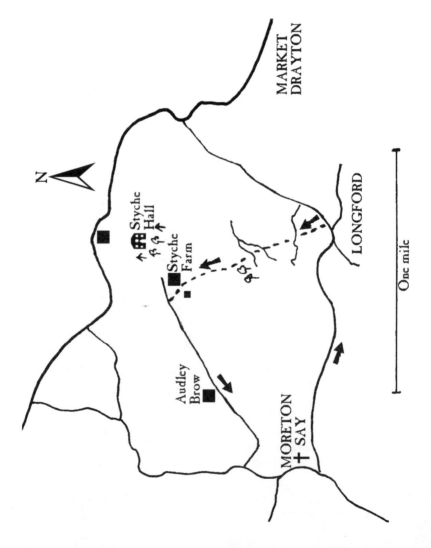

there is a little mystery which I will reveal anon. You may be fortunate to find the church open but, alas, it is more likely to be closed to guard its contents from despoliation and theft from the vagabonds of your day. However, by enquiry you may gain entry and, if successful in this, be mindful to make appropriate contribution towards the preservation thereof.[1]

With your back to the church turn left to a junction then turn left again along a lane towards Market Drayton & Longford. You will need to walk for about a mile before gaining the village of Longford, so let me tell you a little of my early years.

My father, Richard, was not a wealthy man even though he was the local squire. His singular lack of success as a lawyer caused him constant struggle to support his large family (I was one of thirteen children no less), and to maintain Styche, which even then was 200 years old. To my eternal regret I did not aid his disposition. I was what you might call a difficult child. Not only that, my health was delicate and these two attributes did in part result in my parents sending me off to live near to Manchester with my aunt and uncle when I was but two years old.

At school I was mischievous and without the remotest interest in learning. During the time of my attendance at the grammar school in Market Drayton my poor father became increasingly perturbed at the torrent of complaints about my behaviour. Hardly surprising when it had been alleged (correctly) that I had become the leader of a gang running what you would now call a protection racket with local shops! Then there was the famous episode when I climbed up the church steeple in Market Drayton and sat astride a stone gargoyle. How I laughed and jeered at the crowd gathered below who shouted at me to come down. I had in fact got up quite safely by the inner staircase and climbed out over the coping.

Anyway, after brief spells at boarding schools I studied book keeping which, at the age of 18, gained me employment with the East India Company (not on merit I hasten to add – my father knew one of the directors). There followed a most disagreeable sea voyage taking over a year, during which I was seasick, homesick, run aground on the coast of Brazil and rescued after falling overboard before finally arriving in Madras. Due to my father's impecunious state I was also in heavy debt – not the best way to embark upon a new life on foreign shores. It was a desperately unhappy time for me; I made no close friends and fell victim to nervous depression. I was even driven to attempt suicide but this was doomed to failure in accordance with all the aspects of my life so far endured. How I longed to be back at Styche in the bosom of my family: the strictures of my parents would have been nothing compared to the deprivation and loneliness I suffered during my first two years in Madras.

It was in 1746, when I was 21, that events changed dramatically.

As you approach Longford there is a gradual incline alongside a black and white Elizabethan style property on the left, called Longford Old Hall. The attractive Victorian property ahead would not, of course, have been there in my day. Bear round to the left then go almost immediately left again along another lane in the direction of Longslow.

Forthwith you will pass a house on the left beyond which is a waymarked gateway into a field. Once in the field you will get the best view possible of Styche in the trees over to the half right. This is the replacement for the earlier building of my birth although I did finance its construction upon my second return from India in 1762 and inherited it from my father in 1771. Alas, it is not a pretty sight. The square shape is less than interesting and they have painted over the brickwork. I understand it has now suffered the indignity of having been converted into four separate dwellings – poor Styche![2]

Now, bear very slightly right across the centre of the field aiming towards a footbridge on the far side. At certain times this and some of the ensuing fields can be a little boggy for which I can only issue a profound apology. Cross the footbridge and walk alongside a ditched brook on the left then gradually move away from it towards the right side of a clump of trees. Here is another footbridge to cross after which follow the path through a small plantation. After about 100 yards or so there is another footbridge to cross after which you walk alongside the clump of trees. You will have realised, no doubt, that none of these footbridges were here in my day – it was a case of jump across or ride through on horseback!

When you reach the end of the trees strike out diagonally right across the remaining part of the field to the top right corner. This leads you out onto a farm track where you turn left. If you encounter mud on this track, again I offer my profuse apology. Go through a gate towards Styche farm. The official right of way is over the fence and right between the farm buildings but, sensibly, there is a permissive diversion and you need simply to follow the track as it sweeps left then right and, on the far side turn left away from the buildings. Styche is over to the right in trees but cannot be seen from here. How the trees have grown! You go over a cattle grid onto a broad track and turn left.

Where was I? Oh yes, a dramatic change of events. You see the British were not the only ones with interests in India. The French also had designs on establishing their presence and attacked Fort St. George whilst I was working there!

Together with my friend Edmund (Mun) Maskelyne, I was obliged to make an escape disguised as a Moslem and join the East India Company military force where, at last, I found my niche. After peace was restored I returned to my employment as a much changed man, with a taste for the more exiting things in life. The break in hostilities gave me the opportunity to lay the foundation of my private fortune through trading ventures with Robert Orme.

Moreton Say church

The English and the French were never far from each other's throats however and, in 1751, the situation deteriorated and once again I found myself back in the army carrying the rank of Captain. It was agreed that I would set out with a small band of men to capture the fort at Arcot, which was commanded by a local prince sympathetic to the French. The move was a success but my cunning adversary laid siege to the fort for two months and was only defeated after a full scale battle. During subsequent skirmishes I was slashed across the face with a knife and cheated death several times but my reputation was made and I was honoured by being endowed with an Indian name 'Sabut Jung', meaning the Valiant in War.

You pass two cottages, then Audley Brow before the track sweeps right to join a lane, where you turn left. On reaching another junction turn left again back into Moreton Say.

In 1753 I fell ill from wounds received in fighting and was given home leave. Before departing I married Margaret Maskelyne, the sister of my friend and returned to England in far stouter heart than I left it. By dint of my fortune I managed to accumulate enough wealth to pay off the mortgages on the Styche Estate, settle my father's debts and purchase a town house in Berkeley Square.

Before I end let me tell you of the little mystery surrounding my demise in 1774. I was a mere 49 years of age when an overdose of opium, (the drug was taken to ease my discomfiture from stomach complaints you understand) was alleged to have ended my life. The question was – did I take the dose deliberately to terminate my suffering? Or, indeed, did I stab myself in the throat as some would have. Speculation at the time certainly favoured suicide but it would be improper of me to enlighten, positively or otherwise, those living more than 200 years after the event. Suffice to say that I was taken from my abode in Berkeley Square (where I died) for burial in a secret location as suicides were then buried in unconsecrated ground. It was not until 100 years later when work on the floor in Moreton Say church revealed the truth – underneath the floor in the chancel was found my lead coffin! The new floor was laid over the spot and there I rest to this day.

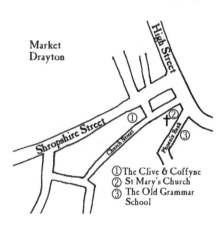

Market Drayton

① The Clive & Coffyne
② St Mary's Church
③ The Old Grammar School

Thus we have come full circle, but I have left out much of the story. Come with me now to my Estate at Walcot...

Notes:

1. The best chances of finding the church open are either side of Sunday services. Otherwise, a telephone call to Rev. Roger Anders at the Rectory on 01630 638110 or Heather Smith on 01630 63857 may be fruitful.

2. No public access to Styche Hall. The driveway is in private ownership.

Bibliography:

Robert Clive, Garrett, Richard, 1976

Shropshire History Makers, Wrenn, Dorothy, 1975

2

The Clive of India Trilogy – 2

1725 – 1774

Maps: Landranger 137 Explorer 216 (mainly) and 201
Start: The village of Lydbury North, 3 miles south-east of Bishops Castle. GR 351860.
Park in any convenient place. Alternatively, you could start from the car park to Bury Ditches Hill Fort, which is located along a minor lane between Bishops Castle and Clunton – see route plan. GR 334839
Walk Distance: 6½ miles
Terrain: Generally easy going. There is an uphill section on the 'second leg' but the views are terrific. Optional climb up to Bury Ditches Hill Fort.
Refreshments: The Powis Arms at Lydbury North. Highly recommended.
Associated places of interest:
1. Walcot is occasionally open to the public. However, appointments can be made at any time but preferably for a group of 20 or more. The gardens and arboretum will be open Fri-Sun from early May through to early Oct. Please tel: 01568 610693 for further information.
2. Powis Castle (National Trust), where the Clive Museum contains a beautiful collection of treasures from India. Clive himself had no connection with Powis but his son Edward, who became the Governor of Madras, married Lady Henrietta Herbert thus uniting the Clive and Powis estates.

The first part of this trilogy covered some of my early years up to the time of my first return from India in 1754. Now I will relate a little of my second spell on the sub continent centred on my estate of Walcot, which I purchased upon my return to this country in 1762.

Find your way back to the main road and turn right along it, passing by an excellent alehouse known as the Powis Arms. If you <u>can</u> pass by that is! (Sorry, that was a poor attempt at humour on my part) You will note alongside what is now the main driveway to Walcot although you cannot see the house at this point. I will apologise now as you need to walk along the main road, which in my day was just a carriage track, for about three-quarters of a mile so please take care as there is no footpath. Those tin boxes on wheels which seem so indispensable to you people are inclined to travel fearsomely fast. The good thing is you are getting the

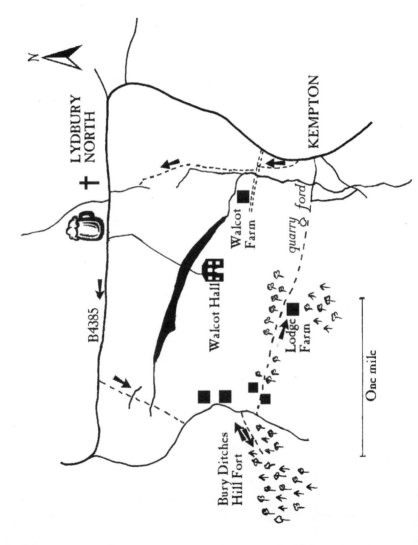

worst bit over with at the start so I will leave you to do it as quickly as possible without distracting you with my verbosity.

You turn left down a waymarked track (you cannot really miss it), which is inclined to get muddy at times, so I hope you are endowed with suitable footwear. You will note that this track is marked the 'Jack Mytton Way'.[1] You will cross a footbridge and another shortly afterwards (again I would remind you that we were not blessed with the convenience of footbridges here in the eighteenth century!) following which the track climbs to meet a lane.

Please turn left along the lane and follow it, mainly in an uphill direction I regret to say, for about a mile. You pass two farms and ignore a waymark to the right shortly thereafter and eventually arrive at the parking place for tin boxes at Bury Ditches Hill Fort. Along the way if you look backwards you will be rewarded by increasingly superb views over Bishops Castle and towards the south Shropshire hills. As you go I will tell some more of my story.

After a year in England I returned to India refreshed, and as Lieutenant-Colonel of Fort St. David no less. Madras was peaceful enough but the French were constantly trying to stir up trouble, particularly amongst the Indian Nawabs. Those people have been a thorn in the side of the English throughout history. As I hope you will understand I have to be selective in what I tell you – a lot of things happened at this and other stages of my life that I cannot possibly go into detail about, so needs must that I confine my comments to the principal events. Oh, but joy of joys! I nearly forgot to tell you that my wife, Margaret, was born of a son in London in 1754 and became pregnant again.

In 1746, Suraj-ud-Daula was the ruler of Bengal and was minded to drive the English out, encouraged of course by the French. He advanced on Calcutta with a large army and those English merchants who had not fled were incarcerated in the garrison prison. There was an overwhelming atmosphere of panic and fear at this time which is difficult for me to convey to you, for it must be remembered that our people were not used to this sort of treatment. Only 23 out of 146 captives survived what became known as the Black Hole of Calcutta, and these were paraded through the streets in chains.

When the news reached Madras I was dispatched with an army to recapture Calcutta and punish Suraj-ud-Daula. The former was accomplished without great difficulty but Suraj had gone into hiding. The position became one of some complexity but, in brief, these events coincided with the outbreak of war again between England and France, which meant that my services would be required in the defence of Madras. However, I could not leave Calcutta at the mercy of Suraj and, after engaging in some subterfuge with his Indian adversary Mir Jafir, I finally defeated him and his French cronies at Plassey. With the loss of twenty-two soldiers killed and fifty wounded I scattered an army of nearly 60,000 and subdued an empire larger and more populous than Great Britain! The Nawab was so grateful that he bestowed upon me land and gifts to the value of £160,000, an immense sum in those days.

By 1760 we had just about finished the French but all this took its toll on my health once again and I returned to England in February of that year.

If you are in the mood for an interesting diversion, and have the legs for it, take the path up to the Fort. It is a stiff climb but I can assure you that, as well as being one of the finest Iron Age hill forts in the land, the views from the top are spectacular. I did not have the benefit of visiting it in its present restored state; indeed I cannot remember that it was accessible at all, undergrowth had been allowed to proliferate unchecked for centuries and there was little, if any, evidence of this historic gem.

A distance of 100 yards past the parking place will bring you to a stile on your left and you cross this onto a track marked Shropshire Way and Wild Edrics Way.[2] The track twists between farm buildings and you go through a gate in front of Stanley Cottage then pass in front of the property to go over another stile onto a broad path amongst trees. Go through two waymarked gates, at the second of which is a National Trust sign for Walcot – 8.2 hectares of the estate having been purchased by that worthy organization in 1994.

Take care over the route now. Very shortly after the second gate – only about 40 yards in fact – there is a waymark post directing you right off the main track down an embankment on a narrower path. At the base of the embankment go ahead on the lower of the two tracks facing you. After a pleasant walk through mixed woodland (I can appreciate why the National Trust purchased it) you pass some cottages adjoining Lodge Farm to rejoin the main track then go through some gates by the farm itself and over a cattle grid to continue on the track. There follows another pleasant section through parkland for half a mile or so where you keep to the track over a stile and pass by an abandoned quarry before going right at a fork towards the settlement of Kempton.

By now I was rich, famous and was to realise my political ambitions by being elected M.P. for Shrewsbury, to serve under William Pitt, who called me his 'heaven born general'. My estate here at Walcot was purchased as was a town house in Shrewsbury[3]. At this stage of my life everything in the garden was rosy, as you would say, but for my health. The damned pain was unbearable though, mercifully, the physician's potions brought me some relief. It was not long, however, before circumstances were to take a turn for the worse. Doubtless some would argue that I had not the constitution for the House of Commons. My support of Pitt was castigated and innuendos were put about as to how I accumulated such wealth as to afford so many residences! In particular, it was alleged that I took money from Mir Jafir by nefarious means – an accusation which cut to the quick I can tell you. I was forced to defend myself against this seditious rumour by the issue of legal proceedings. Perhaps there had been a little subterfuge but it was all means to a just end and my conscience was clear. My enemies included the Chairman of the East India Company, one Laurence Sullivan who pursued a relentless attack on me in Parliament. However, before things could be brought to a head, there came developments in Bengal which demanded my attention.

Ignore a crossing right of way and go through a gate by what was one of six lodges to the Walcot Estate and turn left along a lane which passes between some pretty cottages before it narrows and crosses a ford. Thereafter it degenerates into a surfaced track and meets a main road – again just a carriage track in the eighteenth century. Turn left for about a third of a mile. There is a grass verge on the right. You should ignore a waymark right and, in another 200 yards, cross a waymarked stile on your left into a field. Cross the field diagonally towards, but slightly to the right of, the top right corner.

Cross the stile in the boundary and go forward to cross another stile to walk along the bottom edge of the next field. At the end you go over a fence stile and across a short area of field to reach a driveway running through parkland with an avenue of horse chestnut trees. This is the original driveway to Walcot – which you still cannot see – and if you look right there are the two lodges on either side of the entrance from the Bishops Castle road. Splendid is it not? I can well remember the great comings and goings along here of carriages in which the gentry of that fashionable era rode, all attired with such exquisite taste.

Turn left on the drive and cross the bridge. After about 100 yards and before the next bridge there is a waymark taking you right across a grassed area to the right of a stream. Walcot Farm is over to your left. You soon cross a stile by a gate and continue alongside the stream, go through a gate opening and proceed on the same course in a large field. At the end cross a stile into another large field where you stay on line with the brook. Just after rounding a bend you cross a footbridge followed by a short section of field at the end of which cross a stile into a larger field. Continue the line forward across it aiming to the right of farm buildings ahead.

My hall of Walcot is quite visible over to the left now and you join a fence and tree line to the right of the farm. At the end cross a stile and turn right on a metalled track towards Lydbury North. It is from here that you get perhaps the best view of Walcot.

It makes me sad to think of my days as master of Walcot. I was never quite so happy as I was when resident there, carrying out numerous alterations and indulging my passion for angling in the lake. My architect Sir William Chambers created a fine residence without destroying its essential character.

I must though condemn an act of desecration which took place during your Second World War! The plantation of trees spelling out 'Plassey' was cut down because it was believed they might be a landmark for enemy aeroplanes! Huh, what wimpish vandalism.

Continue along until meeting the main road and turn left back to the village, but visit the church on the way. I think you will find it of interest. The next and final chapter of my story moves to Bromfield, near Ludlow.

Notes:

1 See walk no. 13, based on Jack Mytton.

2 See walk no. 10, based on Wild Edric.

3 Clive House Shrewsbury and his statue can be seen on walk no. 5 – Charles Darwin

Bibliography:

Robert Clive, Garrett, Richard, 1976

Shropshire History Makers, Wren, Dorothy, 1975

Walcot Hall – A Brief History, Parish, Judith,

Walcot Hall

The Clive of India Trilogy – 3

1725 – 1774

Maps: Landranger 137; Explorer 203
Start: The village of Bromfield, three miles to the north-west of Ludlow on the A49. GR 480770. You could park on the former road running alongside the A49 in front of The Cookhouse at the Clive Arms and other buildings adjacent, but please do not obstruct any entrances.
Walk Distance: 6 miles.
Terrain: Well used paths around Ludlow and the picturesque Oakly Estate.
Refreshments: The Clive Arms at Bromfield and numerous places in Ludlow.

Cottages near Dinham Bridge that were named after Clive

In the second part of this trilogy I explained how my sojourn in India brought me fame and wealth but also how my life in England was racked with pain and political intrigue. Now, bear with me as I summon up the fortitude to acquaint you with the final acts.

As with the second part of this trilogy we shall be getting the less interesting part out of the way first – always the best thing to do in any situation really, don't you think? Walk along the main road towards Ludlow passing by a beautiful terrace of half timbered cottages which were there well before my tenure here and cross onto the footpath on

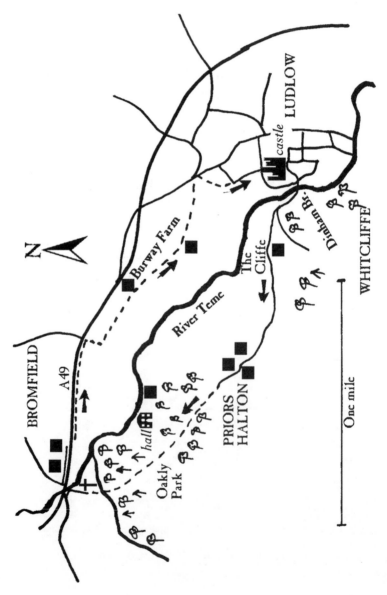

the opposite side of the road. At the risk of repeating myself, this road was a mere dirt track in the eighteenth century and there were more sedate forms of transport using it! You only need to suffer this for about 200 yards before branching off along a waymarked bridleway which runs parallel to the road for about half a mile. At least now you have some protection from the noise of tin boxes.

As I said earlier, developments in Bengal became pressing. The East India Company's financial interests in the province were in a parlous state and there were rumours of a massacre of Europeans at Patna. I was sent to restore order but, I freely admit, that I had no stomach for it, especially as my wife was pregnant once more and was unable to accompany me. I certainly was not well and it seemed to me unnecessary that I should personally attend to these matters. However, attend to them I did, although I say so myself, with ruthless efficiency. Corrupt officials were rooted out and executed or cashiered and proper values restored. I will not bore you with all the details of this but I made some enemies in the process, there is no doubt about that.

My health deteriorated again in December of 1766. A letter to my wife from Major John Carnac said that 'his Lordship has had his mind so continually upon the strain in studying the Company's interest, and his stomach being from the malignancy of the climate overcharged with bile, from both these causes his nerves have been affected in the most violent manner.' Although the Directors would have liked me to stay on for another year my physician, Dr. Ingham, would not hear of it and in February of 1767 I set sail for England once again. I know now that there were many who were happy to see the back of me.

The ravages of ill health had turned me cantankerous, moody and depressed but, though I hardly deserved it, my wife's devotion never faltered. A trip to France restored my spirits[1] for a while and, on my return, I invested further in property including Oakly Park which was sold to me by the Earl of Powis. It was not long before those who were only too willing to heap praise upon me for gaining our empire in India were to turn against me in a vile vendetta.

If you look to the right now you can see Oakly but you will get a much closer view later in the walk. You can also see the prominent feature of Ludlow church tower ahead right. On reaching the next waymark, as I said this is after about half a mile on the track, branch right along the side of a field. For the avoidance of doubt the road off the A49 going back towards Bridgnorth is to your left as you reach the turning point. Ahead now are the woods of Whitcliffe and Mary Knoll, the topography of which has changed considerably since my time here. At the end of the field is another waymark directing you left along the bottom edge of the same field and, at the end of this you go through a waymarked gate before Burway Farm.

You now walk along a broad swathe of grass at the rear of the farm and out onto what can at times be a muddy track. Keep going past a waymark and through another gate before passing some attractive property to the right and crossing the entrance drive to it. Continue onwards towards Ludlow with views of the castle coming up on your right and stay on course as the track turns to tarmac and passes in front of some pleasant houses, all of which are new to me, of course. You eventually meet a junction with a road and turn right along the footpath into Coronation Avenue. After only 100 yards turn off right up some steps and through a kissing gate into a field.

Turn half left in the field heading directly for the castle and on the far side go through another kissing gate and over a little footbridge. Continue ahead across another footbridge and down an alleyway between walls, through yet another kissing gate and out to a junction with a lane.

Here continue forward up though the residential outskirts of the town and stay with it as it bears round to the right. You can see part of the castle wall on your left now and you immediately branch off left down a footpath which takes you around to the rear of the castle and a junction of paths where you turn left up into Castle Square. You may have noticed that you have in fact joined Mortimer's Trail, so named after Roger de Mortimer, a powerful feudal lord in these parts well before my day.

Part of Ludlow Castle today

Ludlow is really a most wonderful place and I recommend you to take a little time to explore. There are plenty of pamphlets available to guide you round. Even just a walk around the market square is rewarding for its historical and architectural interest, most of the buildings having been in existence during my time at Oakly. More of them were just houses then of course, and for the fairly well-to-do, although there were some shops where supplies could be obtained. A visit to the Castle is also worthwhile but you will need a good hour to do it. The Castle was in Crown ownership during my lifetime, having been abandoned after the Civil War. It was described in 1722 as the 'very perfection of decay' and in 1771 it was leased to Lord Powis who subsequently purchased it in 1811. A description applied at that time was a 'picturesque romantic ruin' which attracted many visitors, was praised by writers, eulogised by poets and painted by artists. There is a famous painting by JMW Turner in 1798 of the castle at that time.

When ready to depart and with your back to the castle entrance turn right in front of a number of interesting buildings and past Dinham House tenanted by Lord Powis in 1780 and owned by his brother-in-law (my son) Lord Clive in 1795. You descend past the Chapel of St. Thomas of Canterbury, the oldest remaining building in Ludlow (apart from the castle) down to Dinham Bridge over the River Teme.

Once across follow the road round to the right, from which there is an excellent view back to the castle and just on your left is a row of cottages which were founded in my name (you have to look carefully at the plaque on the front). Where the road swings left uphill continue ahead down a lane signed Priors Halton and The Cliffe Hotel. Ignore waymarks right and left nearby the hotel and stay on the lane for getting on for a mile before reaching the agricultural hamlet of Priors Halton. Now is an opportune time for me to continue my tale.

Laurence Sullivan was in the vanguard of the personal attacks on me which lasted a full five years; also the Johnstone Brothers, one of which I caused to resign from his job in Calcutta. There were others – oh, I had plenty of enemies all right – most of whom believed that I acquired my wealth through dishonest means and exploited the Nawabs for my own ends. Fraud, embezzlement and creating trading monopolies were just a few of the heinous crimes of which I stood unjustly accused.

To cut a long story short, I was forced to defend myself in open debate in Parliament during which my accusers, those contemptible and odious beings, required restitution – I would have to hand over to the state all the money I had obtained in India on the grounds that I had done so illegally! My final speech to the House was, I think, my finest ever and one which extracted every ounce of emotion. 'Take my fortune' I said 'but save my honour'. The next day I learned with the utmost relief that the motion had been defeated and a resolution passed 'that Lord Clive did at the same time render great and meritorious services to his country' At last I had been vindicated.

Continue through the hamlet (the 'Private, No Through Road' sign is just for tin boxes) some of which I remember well, and go out the other side on a broad farm track. Keep on the track past a stone lodge and through a wooded area, after which it rises to a gate. Go round this and continue through an avenue of oaks in Oakly park. It is a beautiful estate would you not agree? You pass a driveway to the stable block and then come around to the house itself, and a pretty good view of it you get too. A magnificent abode I would say without fear of contradiction.

After my ordeal I was appointed Lord Lieutenant of Shropshire. A signal honour indeed. Lady Clive turned Oakly into a happy home and I was content to fill it with paintings although I still spent much time at Walcot and Berkeley Square. Unfortunately the campaign of vilification had preyed upon my already disturbed mind and the bouts of physical pain grew ever more acute. It is said that I became depressed and melancholy and sat in silence for long periods from which nobody could arouse me, not even Margaret.

You pass through a gate by the main entrance lodge – as you will see the estate is now in the hands of the Earl of Plymouth – and cross a bridge with the old mill over to the right. There is an even older mill on the other side of the river which has now surrendered to the elements. I can recall it in full working order so to see it like this saddens me. Progress I suppose. Pass the church of St. Mary the Virgin which is well worth a visit, it is very old and atmospheric. There was once a Priory on the site (some remains are still visible to the right of the church) and the beautiful building fronting the lane was once the gatehouse to it. Now simply continue the remaining short distance back to whence you started.

As you may have read in the first part of this trilogy my life came to a sudden and dramatic end. It was at 3-o'clock in the afternoon of 22nd November, 1774 that my valet found me dead in my bedroom at Berkeley Square.

Speculation attributes a number of possible causes, the most favoured being suicide either by stabbing or an overdose of drugs, but only I know the real cause. As I said my body was taken secretly to Moreton Say; no stone marks my grave, just a tablet set in the wall of the church bearing the Latin inscription 'Primus In Indis'

Notes:

1. Clive stayed at Pézenas in Southern France and liked it so much that he expressed his gratitude in an unusual and enduring way. He handed over the recipe for his petits pâtés, which originated from the kitchens of his home at Styche, near Market Drayton. They are still served in the Clive and Coffyne pub there (see walk 1). Like cotton reels, these tubular little pies were filled with meat (usually mutton), brown sugar, suet and lemon rind and are the great, great, great, great, great grandparents of today's mince pies. The word 'Coffyne' actually means 'pie-case' in early English.

Bibliography:

Robert Clive, Garrett, Richard, 1976

Shropshire History Makers, Wrenn, Dorothy, 1975

Tales of Old Shropshire, Lawrence-Smith, Kathleen, 1991

4

The Darbys of Coalbrookdale

1678, Birth of Abraham Darby I – Death of Abraham Darby IV, 1878

Map: Explorer 242, but not essential.

Start/Park: Car park to The Museum of Iron in Coalbrookdale. You turn right off the river road a mile to the west of Ironbridge and go along the length of the Dale, passing the Coalbrookdale Works on your left. Immediately afterwards fork left and follow the signs to the Museum of Iron car park. GR667048

A visit to the Museum is optional (before or after the walk) but recommended.

Walk Distance: About 4 miles. Please take into account that this should be a very 'leisurely' walk with time given to soak up the immense history of the area, a little of which is set forth in the text (which, of necessity, is longer than normal).

Terrain: Very easy although there is a little effort required to reach The Rotunda, but the view from there is spectacular.

Refreshments: The Coalbrookdale Inn plus others at the bottom of the Dale.

Associated places of interest: Blists Hill and Associated Museum Sites – as the seat of the Industrial Revolution this area is very rich in relics of the age. It is, of course, a World Heritage Site.

For information contact The Ironbridge Gorge Museum Trust, The Wharfage, Ironbridge. Tel: 01952 433522.

Please walk over to the old blast furnace, now enclosed to protect it from the elements, and whilst looking at or around it you may care to read the following introduction.

I expect you will have heard the name Abraham Darby, but did you also know how many members of this pioneering family bore the same name? Well, there were in fact four of us spanning a period of 200 years between the late seventeenth century and the end of the nineteenth. Yes, four Abraham Darbys and not a few other Darbys as well, all of who contributed to a greater or lesser degree to the fortunes of a dynasty which was to be in the forefront of the great industrial revolution that had its beginnings here in Coalbrookdale.

I am Abraham Darby the Fourth and, as the last of the line (there were subsequent Darbys who continued our work but we are really concerned here with the most important period of the Dale's history), it is fitting that I should guide you through this celebrated time and place because I have the full benefit of knowing how events unfolded throughout the lives of my forebears, in such a way that would change the world. I must, however, entreat you to be understanding as I can only provide you with a potted history of such events – anything else would take up far too much room and probably bore you anyway.

The creation of several museum sites in The Ironbridge Gorge to preserve the remnants of the age and to inform people of our magnificent heritage is a most laudable thing and one which gives me great pride As you will by now have realised one of these, the Museum of Iron is close at hand. You can visit this now or at the end (or not at all) but please make a note of opening times and bear in mind that I've got 150 years or so of history to get through!

The story begins with Abraham Darby I, my great great grandfather, and you can see the remains of his pioneering blast furnace right here. This incorporates parts of the original blast furnace in which he first smelted iron ore with coke (instead of charcoal, which was limited in supply) in 1709. Little could he have known that this new process was going to start such a dramatic revolution in the iron industry. There is information available for you to read inside so I won't repeat it here. Have a good look around the outside also – you might be able to imagine the scene here of almost 300 years ago with the heat, noise and dust pervading the air, and the great creaking of the water wheel kept in motion by rushing water from the storage pool above (which you will see shortly).

In the early days production was mainly of cast iron pots and pans but this new process enabled Abraham Darby I to improve quality and quantity although it must have been nigh on another 50 years before it really made an impact on the trade generally. It is the same with anything new – treated with disdain and slow to catch on except with forward thinking people. The beauty of it was that the virtually inexhaustible supply of coke meant that the furnace could be kept going more or less all the time whereas, with charcoal, production had to cease when material was in short supply.

Why Coalbrookdale you may ask? Well, simply because the location met all the criteria necessary to produce good quality iron efficiently and in great quantity. There was a plentiful supply of iron ore, wood to make charcoal, water to power the bellows, limestone and, of course, the River Severn for transport. A canal system linking the South Shropshire coalfield around Wellington (where the raw material for coke making was mined) with the Severn via the inclined plane at Coalport would later improve the movement of goods and materials immeasurably.

There, I've taken up more space than I wanted to just with a brief piece of scene setting. When you are ready, go up the steps facing you as you leave the furnace building, turn right under the viaduct then right again. At the road junction turn left and take the footpath uphill alongside a low wall. You will shortly arrive at Dale House, home to successive generations of Darby's and built by Abraham Darby I (although incomplete at the time of his death in 1717).

Next to that is Rosehill House, also lived in by members of the family but a little later.[1] Close by is another large house called Chestnuts – that's where I once lived. You will also see a sign to the Quaker Burial Ground but we will leave that to the end – fittingly, because that is where most of my forebears ended up, though not me I hasten to add! Oh, did I not mention that the family were Quakers? Well they were, although again I was the odd one out. The black sheep you might say, for I changed to Protestantism for very good reasons. But more of that anon.

You can see, running in an elevated position along the rear of the houses, a row of cottages – called Tea Kettle Row – built in the 1740s for the workpeople. There are other surviving examples of these community cottages later on the walk. Retreat back to the junction but this time follow the lane under the viaduct around the rear and above the old furnace. On your left is what was Upper Furnace Pool, one of a series of six pools created from two small streams flowing into the valley by building dams.

These impounded the water which turned wheels for powering bellows and were a godsend really as they enabled the furnace to keep working even during times of water shortages. In other words the furnace did not have to be shut down in the summer, with resultant benefits in terms of production. All of the pools, apart from this and New Pool nearby, have now unfortunately been filled in and I am not best pleased about the state of the Upper Pool. Still, I expect the cost of restoring it is prohibitive.

Continue walking and you will reach a junction with the road running through the Dale. Cross it directly over a village green area which was the site of the Coke Hearths where coke was made for smelting. On the far side of the green, take the upper metalled road running between the Old School House and a row of cottages known as 'Engine Row'. At the 'No Entry' sign bear left onto a footpath up to New Pool, the only other surviving pool in the original system. If you take a left fork here you will find yourself on the top of the retaining dam.

Tragedy struck in 1717 when Abraham Darby I died after being ill for about two years. He was only 39 and did not survive to occupy Dale House. His son, Abraham Darby II was only six and control of the business passed to Thomas Goldney and Richard Ford, the son-in-law of Abraham Darby I's widow Mary and first occupant of the house. During this period the Company started to make cast iron parts for steam engines and produced the first iron railway wheels. It was not until 1728 that Abraham Darby II started to take an active role, at the age of 17. One of his innovations was the installation of a Newcomen steam pumping engine (on ground below the old mill – opposite the Old School House – if I recall, on what is now a play area) to return water from the lower to the upper pool thus maintaining a circuit of water and render any closure of the works during the summer totally unnecessary. Engine Row was built by Abraham III and named after the successor to the Newcomen Engine – a Boulton & Watt steam engine named 'Resolution' and installed in 1781.

Now return to the main track and retrace your steps for a few yards and take an alley up beside the first house you come to. This shortly brings you out onto a concrete lane where you turn left then almost immediately right onto a public footpath signed 'Church Road'. You are now entering Dale Coppice. The path takes you along the rear of some Victorian cottages then curves left and climbs to meet a long flight of wooden steps at which point you follow the waymarked sign to Church Road. The steps then curve round to the right and then sharply left. At the top continue slightly right and take the waymarked fork right downwards to Church Road then almost immediately branch left at another waymark.

Abraham II perfected the process of making pig-iron to be used in the forges while employing coke in his blast furnaces. The ironwork produced was of a much superior quality. He also acquired the mining rights over vast areas of land in Dawley and neighbouring areas thus providing a source of raw materials for several generations to come. A new blast furnace was built at Horsehay[2] and greater use was made of railways, which the Company could now construct itself with its own products, supplanting the old wooden lines. The ironworking industry had thus become a truly integrated enterprise.

On the outbreak of the seven years war in 1756 there was an upsurge in demand for munitions which the Darby ironworks took full advantage of. This led to the construction of a second furnace at Horsehay and acquisition of further mining rights. On the opening of the second furnace the family provided food for upwards of 300 people. We killed a fat cow, and the fatted calf. There were hams and ten large puddings filled with fruit and two hogs heads of drink. We carried it up in railway wagons and had four tables spread under covers. It was indeed a grand affair.

Abraham II died in 1763 at the age of 51 and his son Abraham III was but eleven years of age. Responsibility for management of the business was assumed by Richard Reynolds, a member of a Bristol Quaker family who had moved to Shropshire and had married the daughter of Abraham II. Reynolds was a talented ironmaster who oversaw a number of important developments in the Company's affairs, including the use of iron rails on the partnership's railways. It was he who introduced what became known as the 'Ironmaster's Paths' or 'Sabbath Walks' which you are on now, their purpose being to encourage the workers to walk with their families on a Sunday rather than languish in public houses. I'm not sure the objective was entirely successful!

Continue the descent until reaching level ground and another waymark where you turn right down a further flight of wooden steps and, at the point where they go right and finally descend to Church Road, turn off them to the left and follow this path signed Rotunda. You may have noticed along the way signs of a former structure in the trees – this was Reynolds House, a sort of retreat from the hustle and bustle of the works. You soon start to climb again up some steps along the route of an old slipway with a gully alongside. Follow it as the surface turns to gravel and loops right in front of an old landslide. Ignore a turning left and continue on the level path to exit via a gate onto a road.

Cross the road directly through a squeeze stile following the Rotunda sign and, if you look right after a few yards, you get an excellent view right along the Dale although you do lose it when the trees are in leaf. In late spring the woodland floor is carpeted with ramson (wild garlic) looking like drifts of snow and arguably making up for the loss of view! Stay ahead at the next waymark and, just before the next one, bear sharp left uphill and after about 50 yards you will reach the remains of a brick and plaster apse. This was once a covered seat placed at a point from which Coalbrookdale could be seen to best effect before vegetation obscured the view. It was here that William Williams painted *An Afternoon View of Coalbrookdale* in 1777 which is now prominently featured in your publicity material for the area.

Now return to the waymark and follow the path ahead towards the Rotunda along the line of Lincoln Hill from which limestone for the smelting process was obtained. At the end of the path you unexpectedly arrive at an open platform some 300 feet above the River Severn giving dramatic views over the Ironbridge Gorge towards the Iron Bridge itself. In fact, you are on the foundations of the Rotunda, once a viewing point with a roof supported on iron columns which was demolished in 1804.

Abraham III (the brother of my grandfather, Samuel Darby) began work with the Company in 1768 when he was 18 and subsequently presided over the most prosperous era of the dynasty, turning it into the largest iron making concern in the land. The enterprise expanded

through the acquisition of more coalfields and the commissioning of further blast furnaces on the banks of the Severn, including Bedlam which you can still visit. The Newcomen engine was replaced with the Boulton & Watt engine known as 'Resolution', probably the largest steam engine to have been constructed in the eighteenth century. To cope with demand ever more furnaces were built, warehouses set up in Liverpool and London and activities expanded into other areas such as farming – which actually was an

Lincoln Hill in springtime

Mike Wootton

*astute move as farms provided many of the horses needed to oper-
ate railways. It provided the ironmasters with influence in the grain
trade, thus enabling them to keep it in the district in times of shortages, thereby ensuring the workers were maintained with a
sufficient supply. Clever people my ancestors!*

*Now, everyone knows about the Ironbridge, that great symbol
of the Industial Revolution which you can see from this
magnificent viewpoint – I hope. This was Abraham III's enduring
legacy to mankind. Its original purpose was to provide a more
convenient crossing of the river for men and materials in this hive
of industry (more convenient than the existing bridge at Buildwas,
that is) and was opened for traffic on New Year's Day in 1781. It
has a span of about 100 feet and contains 400 tons of castings –
equivalent to the output of a blast furnace for over three months!
The time of Abraham III saw Coalbrookdale and the surrounding
area become the premier industrial location in the country and
people from all walks of life flocked here to see for themselves
this new technology which was rapidly transforming their lives.
Sadly, like his grandfather before him, AbrahamIII died young
and also aged 39. The year was 1789.*

When ready to depart, descend the steps to your right, all 150 of them,
to reach the line of a former plateway where you turn right then
immediately left to continue the descent. At the bottom turn left along a
path signed Lincoln Hill Road to the left of a brick wall. This soon brings
you out onto a broad track at which point continue ahead along it, then
right after another 50 yards or so onto a lane and continue until arriving at
the main road. As you walk down this section of lane you can see in the
undergrowth to your right the extensive remains of some former furnaces.

If you wish you can, at this point, walk the mile or so into Ironbridge
itself, then return. Me? I think I would rest my legs in an alehouse before
going any further. To satisfy your thirst turn left anyway towards Ironbridge
where you will find several alehouses alongside the river. Whatever you
decide you will need to turn right up a narrow tarmac lane about 15 yards
past your exit point onto the main road. Ignore a No Through Road to the
right and continue along the lane which runs parallel with the main road
running up the Dale back in a direction towards the starting point. After a
while you pass a large gothic looking residence on the right and,
immediately after that, turn left down a path and some steps bringing you
to Upper Forge. As you will see this has been restored for modern day
commercial use.

*After the death of Abraham III his brother (and my
grandfather) Samuel continued to run operations but he too soon
died in 1796 at the age of 41. Again the succession was thrown into*

*some turmoil as Abraham's son, Francis, was only 13 at that time.
Affairs were handled by the various shareholders within the Darby,
Reynolds and Rathbone families but, unfortunately, the whole
enterprise had now become unwieldy and its reputation suffered.
They revived gradually in the early years of the new century when
my father, Edmund Darby, took control. Bridge building became a
major activity and castings supplied for other bridges, including
Thomas Telford's structure at Buildwas. Steam engines too were
made to the designs of James Watt and Richard Trevithick. This
did not mean that we abandoned our traditional iron houseware –
far from it, the ironmasters found it difficult to keep up with
demand for such goods.*

*The period of the Napoleonic wars was one of prosperity but
this did not last long after the peace of 1815, when the price of iron
began to fall. Furthermore, there was increasing competition from
other ironworks in South Wales and The Black Country. Edmund
Darby died in 1810 and was succeeded by Francis. It was in the late
1820s that I, together with my brother Alfred, began to work for
the Company. We managed to reduce operating costs by also
using slack to fire the boilers and waste products with a high iron
content. Other working practices were changed (not without some
opposition from the men though) and various rebuilding projects
undertaken. New plateways were constructed linking the different
ironworks and we branched out into brick making, roofing tiles
etc. as well as ornamental castings for domestic and artistic use. In
1844 I purchased ironworks in Ebbw Vale and elsewhere in Wales.
Though I say so myself, I did keep Coalbrookdale 'on the map'
and was particularly proud when our art castings were exhibited at
the Great Exhibition of 1851. One of these, a statue of
Andromeda, was purchased after the exhibition by Queen
Victoria!*

Turn right to walk up the Dale and you will pass the Literary & Scientific
Institute founded under my patronage in 1859, now a Youth Hostel. Once
past take the second gateway opening on your right, with a pair of garages
on your right, and go up between the houses and up a flight of steps to enter
the churchyard of Holy Trinity. On your right as you approach the church
you will find my family grave – it is made of white marble and stands out
somewhat! The Church is kept locked but you may be lucky enough to find
it open – if so there are numerous interesting features, including a unique
ceiling painting over the altar.

*You may remember my remarks at the start of the walk about
religion and the Quaker faith – the order to which all my*

illustrious forebears belonged. Why then am I buried in a C of E churchyard? Simple – I changed faith and this church was actually built at my cost and given to the Dale in 1854. There are some who say that my change of faith was prompted by business considerations as many of my customers were of the traditional persuasion and did not understand Quakerism. Well, that is for me to know and you to wonder about!

Go out from the churchyard by the main entrance and immediately pass another row of cottages called Charity Row and continue towards the main road with the Methodist Chapel on the corner. Go to the right of the Chapel and, when you get to some gates into private property cut left down a narrow gravel path to the left of a wall. When you reach the road cross to the footpath on the other side and turn right. You will pass Carpenters Row on the right, built during the time of Abraham III and now, sadly, looking a little neglected. Turn left down Darby Road back to the Museum and car park but, before you finally finish, follow the signs up to the Quaker Burial Ground where my ancestors, or most of them (except Abraham I who is buried at the Quaker cemetery in Broseley) were laid to rest together with William Reynolds and other prominent figures of influence referred to in my story.

I will end now because there is not a lot more to say. After my death in 1878 the business continued although in a contracted form and, of course, is still in operation to this day.

I know that those amongst you with some knowledge of local history will say that I have missed out many salient facts – this is

The grave of Abraham Darby IV   Mike Wootton

undoubtedly true but if I were to include everything you would never finish the walk! I hope you have enjoyed it. For those who wish to know more there is plenty of further information available.

Notes:

1. The Darby Houses are open from Easter to end October, daily. The Dale House opens 10.00 am to 5 .00 pm and Rosehill House from 11.00 am to 5.00 pm. Rosehill House has been restored to show it as it was around 1850 and contains numerous effects of the Darby Family. Dale House was undergoing major restoration work at the time of research. For further information and confirmation of opening times tel. 01952 242420

2. A pool was enlarged to provide sufficient water power to operate the blast furnace and this still exists together with the superb row of cottages alongside called 'Pool View'

Bibliography:

The Darbys of Coalbrookdale, Trinder, Barrie 1991

Coalbrookdale and The Darbys, Thomas, Emyr 1999

The face of Abraham Darby III in the Iron Bridge?

Mike Wootton

5

Charles Darwin – 1

1809 – 1882

Maps: Not essential
Start/Park: The large pay & display car park in Frankwell, Shrewsbury, close to Welsh Bridge. To reach this point it would be best to approach the Town from the west off the A5 via the A458, B4386 or A488, all of which converge at the island in Frankwell.
Walk Distance: about 3½ miles.
Refreshments: You are spoilt for choice in Shrewsbury.
Associated place of interest: St.Chad's Church, Montford 5 miles to the west of Shrewsbury – in the churchyard

is the Darwin family tomb containing the remains of Dr. and Susannah Darwin together with two of their daughters. Charles himself is buried in Westminster Abbey.

No doubt my name is familiar to you. I am looked upon either as the bringer of enlightenment or a loathsome heretic. It all depends on your view of life itself but, regardless of that, allow me to tell you a few things which you may not know. It all began here in my beloved Shrewsbury in 1809.

From the horseless carriage park walk back to the traffic island and keep right, taking the first turning off it to the right along Drinkwater Street. You will, I trust, forgive me if I express some distaste at the vast acreage of tarmac and pollution hereabouts on what was merely meadow and tracks until the advent of your Internal (or should I say Infernal?) Combustion Engine. The town centre itself, which I will take you through later, has also suffered immeasurably from it, although not as badly as some places I fancy.

Statue of Charles Darwin outside the former Shrewsbury Grammar School

Just past the St. George's Church (where my bossy sister Caroline was married and from which point I shall, without modesty, draw your attention to two streets which bear my name that you can see if you take the trouble to walk a little ahead) turn left down Hermitage Walk. You are now approaching Mount House, the place of my birth on 12th February, 1809, although you cannot see it yet. Behind the wall on your right was the kitchen garden and further along the pleasure garden – mostly built on now I'm sorry to say. You continue on an elevated section alongside what is now called the A458. However, it still has the name of 'The Mount' and if you walk a little further you reach a driveway up to Mount House. It is now occupied by a division of the Inland Revenue – something I am not altogether sure I approve of – and you can walk through the gate most times to get a closer look at it. [1]

My father, Dr.Robert Darwin, was an overbearing man in both manner and stature. Standing 6ft 2in. and weighing 24 stones he possessed a dominant presence and had the art of making everyone obey him to the letter. Notwithstanding this he was of jovial temperament if somewhat fidgety and prone to bouts of fatigue. In contrast to his bulk was a high- pitched voice that made him an easy target for mimicry. He came to Shrewsbury in 1786 as a young man of 20 to start a medical practice and soon became so well established that he could afford to marry and build this house. It must be said that he married exceeding well; Susannah, the eldest daughter of Josiah Wedgewood, founder of the famous pottery firm, no less. I was the fifth of six children and the second son of that union which, unfortunately, was to come to a premature end. My mother died when I was but eight years old and although it pains me somewhat, I have little memory of her except her death bed, black velvet gown and a curiously constructed work table.

Continue along the footpath for about 150 yards then turn right down a public footpath between houses, through a wicket gate and down some steps (please be careful, they can get slippery in damp conditions) taking you out into meadows bordering the River Severn[2] Bear right at the bottom along the riverbank, through a kissing gate and then walk alongside the high embankment at the bottom of my garden.

All around here was my playground when a small boy and where I am sure my interest in natural history was born. At this time it was more attuned towards collecting things, especially shells and pebbles of all shapes and sizes, but please do not get the idea that I was an introverted little goody-goody. On the contrary I was something of a prankster and much given to inventing deliberate falsehoods for the sake of causing excitement. I remember once convincing another boy that I could produce various coloured flowers simply by watering them with certain coloured fluids! On another occasion I gathered fruit from trees in our garden and hid them in the shrubbery then ran into the house in breathless haste to spread the news that I had discovered a hoard of stolen fruit.

You continue alongside the river until climbing up some steps before crossing the end of Drinkwater Street to go down an alleyway at the rear of some mainly Victorian houses. At the end turn left and go down some more steps towards the river again, through a kissing gate then out onto an embankment above the river. Stay with the footpath as it winds around to the right towards the town again with a panoramic vista of mainly Georgian properties overlooking the scene, many of which were there during my time. The ugly exception being the product of mid-twentieth century development called a block of flats.

Keep going until you are obliged to negotiate another kissing gate and stay on the riverside path to emerge onto a playing field. Follow the edge of the playing field and you come out into the carriage park again. You could return to your carriage at this point to change footwear as the remainder of the walk is on hard surfaces. Walk out to the very rear of the carriage park (do not cross the blot of a new concrete bridge) and out of the other side along a short section of roadway past a floating eating house (very novel I must say), up the embankment and turn left across Welsh bridge.

This bridge was completed ten years before my birth but I clearly remember my father talking about attending the opening ceremony. Once across, and having crossed to the right hand footpath, you will see directly in front of you a stunning Elizabethan property called Rowley's House, the first brick house in the town, now a museum. Go and look more closely at it by all means but we need to turn right along Lower Claremont Bank. At the top is the massive structure of St.Chad's Church.[3]

It was here that I was baptised in November 1809. I don't remember it. What I do remember is being taught by bossy Caroline and then being sent to the day school of Rev G Case, the Unitarian Minister at No.13 Claremont Hill. Just backtrack a short distance and go down Claremont Hill alongside the church and you will find No.13 on the right – the largest property in the street and little changed to this day. If you now go back to the church and enter the churchyard you will see that the house backs onto it and it was here, at the rear, where the schoolroom was located. I recall vividly watching the burial of a soldier, William Matthews, in August 1817 – I can still see the horse with the man's empty boots and carbine suspended to the saddle and the firing over the grave. Across the road is 'The Quarry' which was used as a playground by pupils of Rev.Case and where I indulged in the study of newts caught in a sunken garden called The Dingle.

On leaving the churchyard turn left and very soon left again into St. John's Hill and at the bottom turn left again into Bellstone. On your left, directly opposite the entrance to the market is Morris Hall. Go into the precincts and you will find the antiquity known as 'The Bellstone'. I was a lad of fifteen when Mr. Richard Cotton first showed me this stone and informed me that there was no rock like it nearer than Cumberland or Scotland. The theory is that it was transported by glaciers but no one really knows although it did kindle a keen interest in me for geology. The entrance to Morris Hall may be closed on Sundays but you can see the stone through the gates. Now I am going to take you on a brief tour around some of the places of interest in my town before showing you my old Grammar School.

Ancient Market Hall in The Square, Shrewsbury

As you exit from Morris Hall Precinct, retrace your steps back along Bellstone and turn left into what is now one of the main areas for shops, which thankfully has been turned into a safe haven from your strange horseless carriages that move at such an alarming rate. Go past Market Street on your right and after a few more yards bear right up an alleyway immediately before the National Westminster Bank. This brings you out into The Square with its ancient market hall built in 1595, although it has not been used as such since 1869. The figure below the old clock of Richard Duke of York came from the old Welsh Bridge and the statue nearby is of Robert Clive of India[4]. At the end of the Hall alongside the Music Hall (I remember this being built because it was the same year as my marriage – 1839) is another passage to venture into known quaintly as Coffee House Passage and, on exit, turn left and after about 30 yards go right along a short cobbled cul-de-sac. At the end is Clive House, so named because Clive of India occupied it during the time he was M.P. for Shrewsbury[4].

Go back to the road and continue along it down College Hill at the bottom of which is a wonderful square of Georgian buildings around a green, sited on which are the remains of Old St. Chad's. When ready to resume go down yet another alleyway (Peacock Passage) opposite the bottom of College Hill. You emerge into High Street and turn left to shortly arrive at the Unitarian Church. Both my parents were Unitarian and worshipped here, along with myself, of course. There is a tablet inside to my memory with carvings representing different subjects of my research. It is a great pity that this and many other churches are kept locked to protect them from vandals and thieves.[5] This was not necessary in my day and I would, in your place, find it extremely irksome.

Retreat back to Peacock Passage and down Bank Passage opposite and, on emergence turn left to reach St. Alkmund's Church built in 1793-5

Statue of Clive in The Square, Shrewsbury

as a replacement for St.Chad's. Go around the side of the church on a cobbled walkway passing in front of Bear Steps Hall which, although presenting a range of arcaded shops, contains a mid-fourteenth century hall restored by Shrewsbury Civic Society in 1969. When you get to the rear of the church turn left down Church Street then turn left again into St. Mary's Street. Cross the road and cut the corner to St. Mary's Church, which is no longer in regular use for worship. The structure is a complex mixture of different materials and styles but is essentially the only medieval church in Shrewsbury centre.

Aim for the Yorkshire House alehouse and turn right towards the former nurses home, now converted into residences, then bear left into Windsor Place. You pass Windsor House on the corner, a fine Regency style building with its classical Ionic doorcase then Perche's Mansion on your left with its 85 ft. long timber framed wall dated 1581. Turn right into Castle Street and shortly left into School Gardens and you will, after a few yards arrive at the former Shrewsbury Grammar School, now used as the public library.

It is to be hoped that you will not fail to notice my statue outside the building! As you face it the dormitories to which I was assigned are located to the left and are now converted into offices.

I was sent to the Grammar School in 1818, following in the steps of many distinguished personages before me, not the least of which was 'Hanging' Judge Jeffreys[6]. My father thought I should become a doctor like him (father, not Judge Jeffreys) but it was I'm afraid a forlorn hope. The curriculum was purely classical and a complete waste of time as far as I was concerned. Life was primitive and discipline harsh although, as a boarder, I did have the significant advantage of being able to visit home on a frequent basis. The Headmaster, Dr.Butler, had a very low opinion of my abilities and I was often rebuked for taking an interest in things like chemistry and 'wasting my time upon such useless subjects'. I actually acquired the nickname of 'Gas' because of the chemistry experiments in the shed at Mount House with my brother.

Outside of school I pursued my interest in natural history as well as developing a passion for shooting. Thereby commenced numerous visits to the home of my Wedgewood cousins at Maer Hall where I could indulge myself to the full. How well I remember killing my first snipe – my excitement was so great that I had much difficulty in re-loading my gun from the trembling of my hands. Even though I say so myself, I became quite a good shot. I was taken away from Shrewsbury School at age 16. My father said that 'You care for nothing but shooting, dogs and rat catching and you will be a disgrace to yourself and all your family' An untypical outburst in point of fact but father was still so determined that I should become a doctor that he sent me to Edinburgh University.

The Castle opposite is well worth visiting if you can spare the time. I won't go on about its history as you can discover that for yourself. When ready to depart continue down the hill and keep going until you reach the river again, at which point you turn left to return to the start.

Edinburgh was just as much a waste of time as Grammar School. The teachers were hopeless and I found anatomy lectures repulsive. Of the two operations I witnessed one was so horrifying that I ran away from it and the memory haunted me for a year. More of my time was spent in the museum studying marine life than attending medical lectures. The warm affection I received at Maer compensated for the strictures of both school and university life and I became particularly fond of my cousin Emma and uncle Jos. There was much agreeable company and I could go shooting as often as I liked. Life was free and idyllic there and left a vivid picture on my mind which lasted forever.

My father gave up hope of my becoming a doctor and next proposed I should take the cloth rather than degenerate into an idle sportsman. For this I needed a university degree and I was packed off, in 1828, to Christ's College Cambridge. The second part of my story is centred on Maer – I know that is just across into Staffordshire but you must forgive this little departure from my beloved Shropshire in order to give better effect to the tale.

Notes:

1.Mount House. It may be possible to arrange internal viewing during working hours but only by prior appointment with The District Valuer and Valuation Officer.

2.The Severn Way. The sign here tells you that this is 'Doctor's Field' but it is not clear whether this is after Dr. Darwin or from some other origin.

3.Church not normally open except around times of services. Built some twenty years before Darwin's birth following collapse of the old church in 1788 – see text.

4.See Clive of India walks no's 1,2 and 3.

5.Unitarian Church. Best chance of on internal viewing is either side of services which are 10.30 and 6.30 on Sundays and 7.30 on Thurs.

6.Judge Jeffreys – see walk 11

Bibliography:

Charles Darwin in Shrewsbury, Shrewsbury & Atcham Borough Council.
Darwin Lifelines, Fletcher, F.D, 1975
Charles Darwin, Chancellor, John, 1973
The Voyage of Charles Darwin. His autobiographical writings, British Broadcasting Corporation, 1978
Charles Darwin, Shrewsbury's Man of the Millennium, Quinn, Henri, 1999

Charles Darwin – 2

1809-1882

Maps: Landranger 127 and 118 Explorer 243 and 257
Start/Park: The village of Maer which is located just off the A51/A53, about 7 miles north-west of Stone and a similar distance north-east of Market Drayton. GR793382.
The Village Hall at the southern end of the village may be a good point from which to start.
Walk Distance: 5½ miles
Refreshments: None on the route

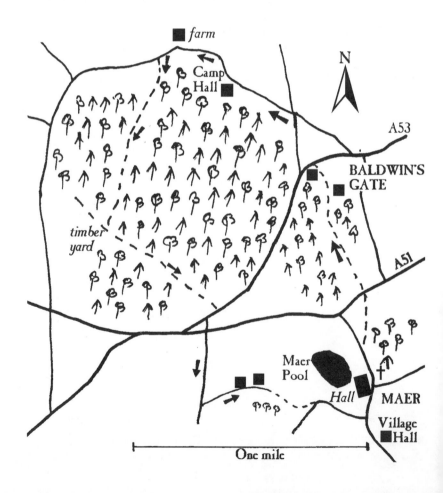

Now, I was telling you in Shrewsbury that my father sent me to Cambridge to study to become a priest. This diversion was also a complete waste of time – more than a waste in fact. I confess, to my shame, that I did the minimum of work – instead I joined the sporting set which included some dissipated, low minded young men. Sometimes I drank too much or ate and drank too much at the 'Gourmet Club' or played cards. Anything except study a subject in which I had not the remotest interest. Mind you, my love for natural history steadily increased; in particular my beetle collection grew extremely large and quite valuable. I remember one day tearing off some old bark and seeing two rare beetles. I seized one in each hand then saw a third and new kind, which I could not bear to lose so I popped the one in my right hand into my mouth. Alas it ejected some intensely acrid fluid which burnt my tongue so that I was forced to spit the beetle out, which was lost as well as the third one.

The village of Maer contains many attractive old buildings, not the least of which is the Hall, the scene of so many happy memories for me as a young man. You need to walk through the village and alongside the Hall and out under the sandstone bridge which leads from the churchyard across to the Hall. After you emerge, go through the timber gate on the right into a field and move away from the left boundary in the direction of a gate on the top boundary, to the left of a line of trees.

Go through the gate and up to what is now a busy road called the A51, cross it carefully and go though a gap on the opposite side into a large field. The correct way is directly ahead across the open field keeping roughly equidistant between wooded mounds on each side walking firstly just to the left of a lone sycamore and then about 20 yards to the left of an oak – however; if the field is planted you may prefer to consider walking around the right edge. Either way you will arrive at a waymarked fence stile in a crossing boundary.

Having negotiated that, stay with the fence line on your right and shortly enter onto a track leading through a gate and on past a large renovated cottage. There are views of the village of Baldwin's Gate down to the right as you continue on the driveway to reach another road, this time called the A53. Cross over to the footpath opposite and bear left for about 120 yards before turning off right down a lane signed Aston and Madeley.

One good thing came out of Cambridge which was to prove instrumental in dictating the course of my life. My interest in natural history enabled me to forge a friendship with J.S.Henslow, a young Professor of Botany and we took to taking long walks in the country together. In fact I became known as 'the man who walks with Henslow'. I left university in 1831 with the most basic degree and embarked upon a tour of North Wales before joining the Wedgewoods for the partridge shooting season. Upon my return on 29 August to The Mount there was a letter awaiting me from Henslow inviting me to join HMS Beagle as the official naturalist on an expedition to survey the coasts of South America.

J S Henslow

Henslow himself had declined the opportunity because of his wife's opposition. I was consumed with joy but feared that my father would not agree to the proposition. How right I was! The post was unpaid and father was convinced that there must have been something wrong with it or the ship if no one else had taken it. In utter despair I wrote to Henslow turning the job down on the grounds of my father's resistance and left for Maer to console myself with partridge shooting.

The very lane you are walking along now and the Maer Woods adjoining were favourite haunts of mine for the sport – I would lose myself for hours and time seemed to become irrelevant. So much so that there were occasions when my hosts became quite anxious about my prolonged absences. On reaching a crossroads after about a third of a mile, turn left towards Aston along another, more leafy lane, passing by Camp Hall on the left with its splendid show of rhododendrons in May. The lane climbs steadily then levels off where views open up to the right over North Staffordshire and Cheshire, then to the left over Shropshire towards Wales.

Maer Hall

The lane goes through a sharp left bend and in another 150 yards or so, and opposite a farm driveway, turn off left through gates onto a broad shaled track leading towards Camp Wood. The track bears right over a stile by a gate, after which stay on the track and keep right at a fork to enter attractive mixed woodland. Ignore all side paths until you come to the next major fork, where you keep right again. You will reach a junction where you go right yet again and stay on this track now (still ignoring all side paths) until you emerge into a timber yard.

My uncle Jos was astonished that I had declined this opportunity of a lifetime and at once set off for Shrewsbury with me in tow to confront my father. He demolished all father's objections, the latter declaring that uncle Jos was, without doubt, the most sensible man he had ever met and there was nothing he could do but give his consent. Thus was set in train a course of events which would revolutionise thought on the origin of mankind itself.

After a miserable wait of three months, during which I became ill and nearly had to withdraw from the voyage, we finally set sail on 27 December 1831. I took an instant liking to Captain Fitzroy even if he was at first alarmed at the shape of my nose! He was a man who commanded respect but his fits of depression were to end in his suicide thirty-four years later. Although treated by the ship's company as a landlubber and frequently had my leg pulled, it was generally good humoured and I got on very well with them.

I cannot begin to tell you of what was to follow. It was simply the most amazing, the most astonishing, the most stupendous, the most awe inspiring, the most wonderful voyage of discovery that anyone has ever had the privilege to be a part of. Mark you, it had its times of privation, but I will gloss over that because it is of little real consequence. The planned three year voyage in fact lasted for five during which we circumnavigated the globe. From South America and round Cape Horn (the roughest voyage imaginable in bitter winter conditions) to the Galapagos Islands and on to Australia followed by Cape Town, finally landing in Falmouth on 2 October 1836.

Now please take care over direction here. You need to turn sharp left through the timber yard keeping left of the open sided store and, after a few more yards, ignore a fork to the right and continue along a path through another section of woodland. Where the wood ends and the path loops left go straight ahead over a stile into an open field. The route is now directly across, past one lone oak to another on the far boundary; however, if the field is cropped it is not difficult to work your way around the right

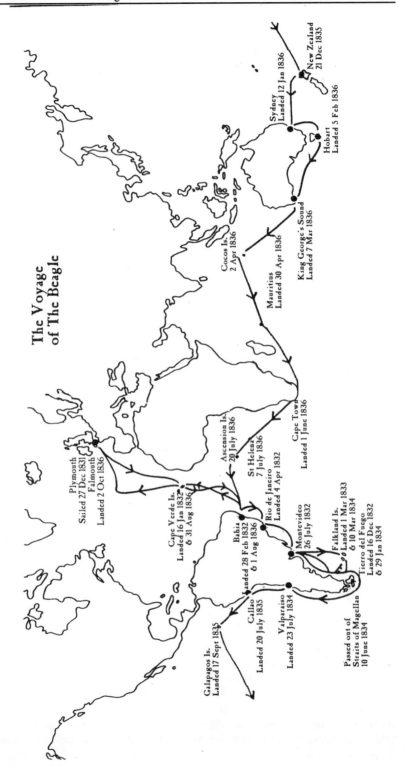

The Voyage
of The Beagle

boundary to the same point, although you will still have to cross a section of the field at the end. You exit via a rough stile onto the road and turn right onto it. This is a busy road so take extra care for the 150 yards or so until you branch off left down a short lane then cross directly over another main road into Wharmadine Lane. Follow this now for about one third of a mile and turn left at the first junction along a very minor lane.

It was in the desolate and hardly known lands of Argentina that the discovery of strange fossilised bones started the early stages in the formulation of a theory that would shake the world. What were these bones? Certainly they were of extinct animals but far bigger than any I knew. I began to ponder on whether species were really constantly developing in a continuous process rather than having been created by some divine intervention as, of course, most people believed. I experienced many wonderful adventures in South America which space will not permit me to relate (you can always purchase a book though!) but I will just tell you of the time I was engaged on an exploration in Chile when I felt the earth tremble. When I later entered the port of Talcahuano I was horrified at the scale of devastation caused by the earthquake. The earth had visibly moved to the extent that the water line was now several feet lower than before. Was this an explanation of why fossils of sea creatures are found thousands of feet above sea level?

The visit to the Galapagos Islands provoked yet more startling ideas. Each island in this small group had its own species of animals and birds which seemed to have adapted to the particular environment and conditions on it. For instance, the birds on one island had strong beaks for cracking nuts but on another beaks were smaller to permit the catching of insects. On yet another the birds were adapted to feed on fruit. There were other examples of the same phenomenon and it became clear to me that the competition for survival had led to this adaptation and development. Moreover, was man himself a product of the same mutability?

You will pass by some isolated cottages and, where the surface ends, continue ahead on a grassy track though a waymarked gate. On reaching a corrugated metal building and yard, pass to the right of it (I am assuming it will still be there when you do this walk but, of course, it may not be! Anyway the general direction is ahead) and once beyond it cross a stile into a field. Keep to the right banked boundary as it loops right to take you over a stile into another field. The area around this gate is sometimes very muddy, so I hope you are wearing sensible footwear. Follow the obvious track veering left alongside a long abandoned greenhouse parallel with the wood on your right. This leads you up to a stile and gate quickly followed by another which gives exit onto a lane where you keep left.

When I reached home again my father was much astonished at the change in my character from an indolent young man to one of a mature, purposeful nature. I am pleased to say that the public soon became eager to hear about my adventures and I was much in demand as a lecturer. In 1839 my journal of the voyage became a best seller. Also in that year I married my cousin, Emma Wedgewood (shooting was not my sole reason for so many visits to Maer!) and she proved to be the ideal companion for the rest of my life.

As you walk along you get sneak views of the back of the Hall and its very pleasant surroundings where I spent many happy days in the company of good friends. They were to stay strong in my memory for the rest of my life. When you get back to the village go back to the Church and you will see in the entrance porch a copy of my marriage certificate. Yes, of course, I married here at Maer but some of you might have realised this already.

Shortly after my marriage I became stricken with an illness which was never really to be cured and in 1842 we moved to the drier climate of Kent. My theories continued to develop and publication of 'The Origin of Species and Descent of Man' caused the greatest controversy of the time and a storm of protest, particularly from the religious among the populace, which was most of them. There were accusations of blasphemy and for a time my family felt like moral degenerates before my theories gained wide acceptance. The rest, as you would say, is history.

Bibliography:
Charles Darwin in Shrewsbury, Shrewsbury & Atcham Borough Council.
Darwin Lifelines, Fletcher, F.D, 1975
Charles Darwin, Chancellor, John, 1973
The Voyage of Charles Darwin. His autobiographical writings, British Broadcasting Corporation, 1978
Charles Darwin, Shrewsbury's Man of the Millennium, Quinn, Henri, 1999

7

Caractacus

First Century

Maps: Landranger 137;Explorer 217
Start/Park: Anywhere convenient in All Stretton, which is located one mile to the north of Church Stretton on the B4370. Alternatively, if you would prefer to have a pub break *en route*, start from the lane running along the northern tip of The Lawley. To get there from the south, continue on the A41 past Church Stretton towards Shrewsbury and, after about four miles at Leebotwood, turn right then left at a junction after another half a mile. A further mile and a half will bring you to a crossroads where you bear right and continue for almost another mile to where the lane twists around the base of the hill. There are some parking areas here and one actually on the bend of the lane where the path joins it. Travellers from the north will, of course turn left at Leebotwood. GR506992. I have started the route from The Lawley end but the choice is yours.
Walk Distance: 10 miles. Please note that this is a fairly long walk with some stiff climbs. It should not be undertaken unless you are fit. It can be shortened or even done in two stages.
Terrain: Mainly up hill and down dale in some of the best of Shropshire Hill country. Magnificent views from several places. *Please see note above.*
Refreshments: The Yew Tree at All Stretton.

No. I was not a Roman – Caractacus was the name they gave to me and I hated it! My real name is Caradoc and you will still find it in use today, mainly in the area you call Wales. Of course, Wales did not exist then; well it did exist but it wasn't called Wales. Most of the towns and villages along the route I am taking you did not exist either, or if they did it was merely as a group of mud huts.

Take a path going from the back of the parking area. Soon cross a fence stile to walk upwards through a belt of trees. This soon broadens out into a grassy swathe climbing steadily up towards the top of Lawley Hill. Splendid views unfold around you. Looking back the Wrekin erupts from the wide expanse of the Shropshire Plain. Clee Hills are off to the left. After a while Caer Caradoc, my hill,[1] looms in front with the Long Mynd curving round to the right with Church Stretton below it. Hope Bowdler Hill is half left and, on a clear day, you can see the Stiperstones with the Devil's Chair at the back of Long Mynd.

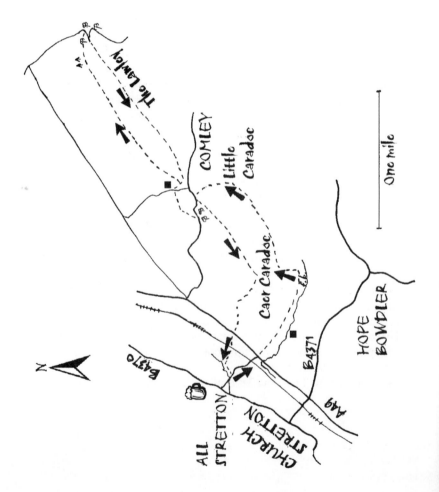

I lack some linguistic finesse, please bear with me. What would you expect from a first century British savage? We were backward, of that there is no doubt and the Romans brought with them great knowledge and a strange culture which we Britons could not understand. Our lands were ruled by many separate tribal leaders and it was because of this that the invaders conquered us so easily. There was very little co-operation between them and each one acted in his own interests even if that meant consorting with enemies. Anyway, my kingdom of the Silures was an area north of what has become your capital and was shared between myself and Togodumnus, following the death of our father Cunobelinus[2]. Our seat of rule was Colchester and it was from here that we led resistance to the Romans when they came in force in AD43.

Damn Claudius. Why could he not have left us in peace? Well, peace is not really the right word. The tribal leaders were constantly at each other's throats to achieve supremacy or territorial advantage but, for all that, I was not going to stand by and be taken by some foreign race without putting up a fight. Although I say so myself we scored some spectacular early successes and gathered support when news of our heroic deeds became known. By waging what you might now call terrorist action we kept resistance going for a full nine years, but in the end it was to no avail.

When you have regained your breath, start descending by going forward on a well trodden path, and have a care on the loose stony parts. Go through a gate at the base of a hill, then forward over a crossing track and down a short section of grassy bank to join and go ahead along a farm track. Shortly bear left in front of a dwelling to reach a lane. Cross this lane following a waymark up steps through a gate into a field following the left boundary. At the end cross a fence stile into the adjacent field but now to the left of the boundary hedge. At the end of this field cross a stile into the next field and go diagonally over it half left to a gate which you can see on far boundary. There is an oak in the middle which you pass. Cross a stile to the right of the gate onto a lane and turn left.

After a short stiff climb, and as lane begins to level out, take a waymarked right turn (sharp right) onto a broad track through trees. Go through a waymarked gate and stay ahead on a nice path through fringe trees at the base of Caer Caradoc. Buzzards and ravens are frequently seen here. The path narrows to go through quite dense vegetation. Keep ahead past a stile on the right and go through a gate onto a well used path. Ignore another stile on the right. After a little climb the ground flattens out a little. You ignore a marker post and continue ahead. As you follow the path through bracken you move away from a fence on your right. Eventually, the way rejoins the fence and you come to another stile on the right which is crossed into a field where you walk down the side of the right boundary to the next stile about 100 yards ahead. Cross and stay on this line in the next field and at the end go through the left hand gate onto a track in a tree belt. Emerge into a field and cross directly to a stile on the opposite boundary, exiting onto the main thoroughfare.

Cross this carefully and avoid covered chariots travelling fast. Go over a stile on the other side into a field. Bear slightly left to a stile on the far side below an embankment to a line carrying huge chariots for many people. Cross the line and a stile on the other side into a field. Go half left cutting off the left corner at the rear of a dwelling, cross a stile in a hedge and turn right onto a narrow path between hedges. This soon broadens out and you come to a footbridge on your right but do not cross it – keep on track and you will come to a lane in All Stretton. Turn right, then right again down Farm Lane and right yet again on reaching road. A short distance will bring you to the Yew Tree drinking house.

On leaving turn right and go back the way you came, left into Farm Lane then left at the junction with Starr Lane past the exit point onto it on outward route. Stay on the lane to cross a bridge over a huge chariot line again. On reaching the main thoroughfare cross diagonally right to go over a stile into a field. Follow the left boundary of trees and at the top corner cross a stile into the next field and another after a few yards, with a farm on the right and fishing pools at the rear. Keep close to the left boundary which slowly loops left. As you get to the end of the field there is a stile on the left which you cross and turn right to continue the same line to the left of a fence in an elevated position above another pool.

Go through a gate by a further pool and shortly after cross a stile by a gate onto a narrower path through attractive wood with a little brook on right. As the wood thins out you will see a footbridge across the stream. DO NOT CROSS IT! At this point the path you are on splits in two. Take the narrower, left one and go ahead as it slowly climbs. In about 85 yards there is a loose scree path on the left that climbs upwards in a series of steps. Turn up here and stay on the upward course as the path changes from stone to grass.

This is a very steep climb but views start to open up over surrounding countryside. After a while you can see stile ahead. Cross and keep upwards. It becomes a little less steep as you approach a rocky outcrop. As you near the top magnificent views open up on right. On a clear day you can see across what have become Wolverhampton and Dudley. The ditches and ramparts of the hill fort are visible ahead of you on the left slopes. At the top are stunning vistas all round. The Lawley stretches out in front with the Wrekin beyond[3]. I am sure you are now ready to take a rest so I will at this point relate to you what happened here almost 2000 years ago.

Inevitably our victories were followed by defeat. It was in the area now called Kent and we were forced to retreat into the (Essex) countryside. The victorious Romans under Aulus Plautus foolishly pursued us but we knew the land and it was not easy to cross. Imagine our delight therefore when, having suffered defeat by them, we were able to inflict damage by picking them off and send them scurrying away with their tails between their legs! Claudius was furious and came himself with more men and a host of elephants, no less. He captured our town of Colchester and we fled to Wales, from where we waged a series of raids across the border.

Ostorios Scapula replaced Plautius and consolidated the invader's hold on the west of Britain. We had good friends in the Cornovii tribe of Shropshire and took refuge with them at the six acre ancient hill fort you are now standing in, or perhaps you haven't reached it yet. You have to continue along the bumpy ridge for a while before reaching the summit and the fort. It is a wild and windswept place for much of the time, with steep slopes difficult for invaders to climb. Also, the rocky outcrops provided us with platforms from which we could hurl stones and arrows down on attackers.

The Roman legions came to the hill[4], and took fright at its formidable appearance. I urged on my men that the work of that day would be the beginning of new liberty or of eternal slavery, appealed by name to their forefathers who had driven back the dictator Caesar, by whose valour they were free from the Roman axe. While I was speaking the host shouted applause; every warrior bound himself by his national oath not to shrink from weapons or wounds.

Such enthusiasm confounded the Roman General. The ramparts on top of the frowning hilltop, the stern resistance of fighting men everywhere apparent, daunted him. But his soldiers insisted on battle exclaiming that valour could overcome all things. Then the Prefects and Tribunes, with similar language, stimulated the ardour of their troops. Ostorius, having ascertained by a survey the inaccessible and the assailable points of the position, led on his furious men and formed a military testudo to tear down our ill compacted defence barrier of stones. After that it was equal hand to hand fighting and we were forced to retire to the fort. You see, we were no match for the Romans in manpower or weaponry.

Even at the fort, both light and heavy armed soldiers rushed to the attack, the first harassed us with missiles while the others closed with them and broke our ranks, destitute as we were of plates and helmets. When the Auxiliaries were brought into the fray our gallant soldiers were cut down by sword and javelin or, if we wheeled round, were again met by sabres and spears. The valour of my men was magnificent and they fought until the hillside ran red. The clash of steel was deafening and the cries of injured and dying men broke my heart. Worse still, my wife and daughters were taken prisoner although I managed to escape and hide in a cave on the western side of the hill.

In utter desolation I went north to the land of the Brigantes and sought protection from their Queen Cartismandua. She, sensing that it was no longer advisable to hold out against the invader, committed the ultimate act of treachery and gave me up to the Romans.

Now starts the great descent. Continuing your original line leave the fort along a well worn path. As the ground becomes less steep you join a fence on the right which takes you down to a stile. Cross it and ignore a waymark pointing left and stay on an indistinct path across the grass towards another rise in view – Little Caradoc. You don't need to climb it but strike off right downhill aiming just to the right of a triangular group of trees in the valley below. You reach the trees and a narrow crossing path. Turn left here and after a short distance right through a gate onto a broader track.

On reaching a lane turn right. It twists and turns passing through the settlement of Comley, after which turn left at a junction. After about 250 yards you reach Comley Park and turn right along a section of the outward way. Follow a waymark around to the right. Cross a barrier for cattle but now depart the outward way by continuing along a broad track. Unless you want to go back along the top of The Lawley again that is! This would have meant nothing to me and my men but I dare say you twenty-first century people might be a little too tired for it now. Anyway, you shortly go through a gate onto a broad grassy track and follow it around the base of the hill.

We were all taken to Rome where news of my valour had gone before me. I was indeed a celebrity and aroused the curiosity of the citizens. We were put on show in some sort of victory parade and huge crowds gathered to see these strange fighters from foreign lands who had dared resist the might of Rome. I was determined to hold my head up high and not appear as a downcast, defeated figure. I had fought a good fight and earned the respect of the victors so I had nothing to be ashamed of. My body was almost naked and painted with figures of beasts. I wore a chain of iron around my neck and another around my middle. Difficult to maintain dignity in such circumstances I think you will agree. Eventually, the procession came before the seat of the Emperor Claudius but, although my life was at stake, and those of my family, I would not beg for mercy.

I addressed the Emperor thus: 'Had my moderation in prosperity been equal to my noble birth and fortune, I should have entered this city as your friend rather than as your captive. Nor would you have disdained the alliance of one descended from illustrious ancestors, and sovereign over many nations. My present condition, disgraceful as it is to myself, reflects glory on you. Possessed as I once was of horses, men, arms and wealth, what wonder is it if I parted from them with reluctance. Had I sooner been betrayed, I had neither been distinguished by misfortune nor you by glory. But if you now save my life I shall be an eternal monument of your clemency'.

This worked well and Claudius granted pardon to me, my wife and my family. We remained in Rome in the highest esteem. I myself died without returning to my native land but my children were converted to Christianity and returned to Britain to spread the faith to which they had become attached. My son, Cyllin and daughter, Eigen, are both ranked among the British saints. One of my other daughters became the wife of a Roman Senator.

When you cross another barrier for cattle you know you are nearly back and when you exit onto a lane you are.

Notes:

1. There are two hills of the same name, the other being near Clun.

2. Made famous in Shakespeare's 'Cymbeline'

3. The three hills can now clearly be seen to be on the same line of volcanic eruption that occurred about 800 million years ago.

4. Caer Caradoc is not the only hill to lay claim to be the site of Caractacus's last stand. Others, such as Breidden Hill near Welshpool, Coxall Knoll at Bucknell and Llanymynech Hill, as well as the second Caer Caradoc all have varying degrees of validity. After nearly 2,000 years it is difficult to determine the exact location, although archaeologists are still trying to do so.

For the purposes of our story, however, there is no doubt in my mind – you only have to sample the atmosphere here to know it is the correct spot!

8

Thomas Telford - 1

1757 - 1834

Maps: Landranger 126, 117; Explorer 256

Start/Park: Public car park in the centre of Chirk, which is just across the border into Wales. In fact, the entire walk is in Wales but that has to be in order to tell the story to good effect. GR 292377

Walk Distance: 9½ miles

Refreshments: The Telford Arms at Froncysyllte, the Last Pub in England and various in Chirk

Associated places of interest:

1. Telford. A 'New Town' and now one of the major population centres in Shropshire. Named after the famous engineer because of his associations with the county.

2. Viriconium (Wroxeter) situated on the B4380, about five miles south-east of Shrewsbury. The remains of this Roman town were discovered beneath farming land and it was Telford's intervention which prevented them from destruction. Now in the care of English Heritage and open to the public. Tel: 01743 761330

3. The churches of St. Michael's, Madeley (to the south of Telford) and St. Mary's, Bridgnorth can be visited although may be locked at certain times.

4. The Longden Aqueduct at Longden on Tern which is some four miles to the north-west of Wellington on the B5063.

I would inform those who are unaware of my origins that I am not a Salopian. I am not even English, but a Scot born in the village of Glendinning in Dumfriesshire in 1757 and I returned there as often as my work permitted in order to visit my family and friends. My association with Shropshire and adjacent areas is, however, extensive – so much so that I have the honour of a town being named after me! Shropshire is, therefore, my adopted county and, indeed, I was working there on my last major project at the time of my death.

From the car park go back to the main street (Watling Street), cross and go down Station Avenue past the memorial to your 20th century wars. As you walk down, the huge blot of a chocolate factory looms up on your right – you will probably smell it before you see it. I suppose it had to go somewhere but I would have preferred it not to have been put next to my canal! Go past the entrance and over the railway bridge, immediately after which you can look down on the section of canal we will walk along later. The canal actually disappears through the Chirk tunnel here and emerges at my aqueduct, but more of this in due course.

Shortly after the bridge take the waymarked path on the right through trees. You can probably see the 'back' entrance to Chirk Castle from here, which as you may know is now a National Trust property [1]. Follow the waymark up some steps, then bear left to continue on a path which takes you down through a kissing gate and across a field. At the end, go through another kissing gate and turn right on a lane.

My father was a humble shepherd and, tragically, died shortly after my birth and this forced my mother to seek charity from her brother. You can still visit what remains of my birthplace and see the gravestone at Westerkirk (Bentpath) which I carved myself in memory of my father. Indeed, my first employment as an apprentice stonemason assisted me in no short measure to do this. Unfortunately, this was not a happy experience and I was lucky to gain another position as apprentice to a Langholm mason, Andrew Thompson. There was good work here which stood me in good stead for the future. The most important was construction of a new bridge across the Esk in 1778. Somewhat to my amazement the bridge still stands.

By the time I was twenty-three I decided that I must seek greater experience and proceeded to Edinburgh. The elegance of the City's buildings awakened an interest in architecture and, after a brief stay in Eskdale, I set off two years later to London on horseback to make a career as an architect and planner. My experiences in Edinburgh had prepared me well for the wonders of

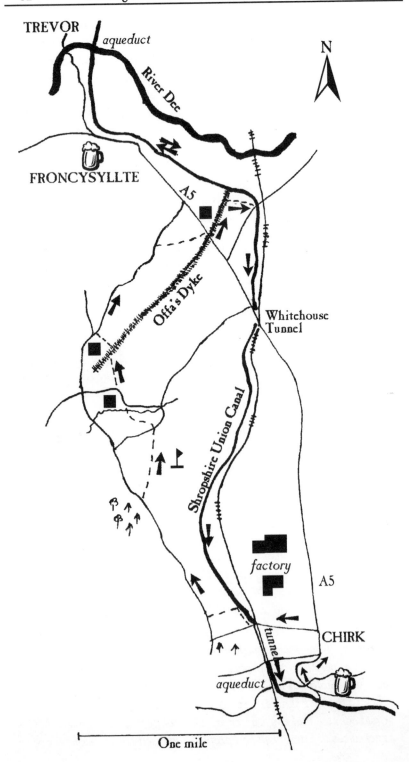

this great city, so at least I was not a country bumpkin lost in a world of splendour and riches. I was also fortunate to have letters of introduction from Mrs Pasley, a Langholm lady of substance who had taken some interest in my progress, to her brother who was a merchant in London. He in turn put me in touch with two great architects, Sir William Chambers and Robert Adam who employed me on their current project of building the new Somerset House.

After about half a mile the lane goes into a left bend and here turn off right up an embankment and over a waymarked stile. Walk along a field edge adjacent to a golf course (not there during my time although the game originated in the fifteenth century) and cross a stile into the next field and go ahead directly on the same line to another stile on the opposite boundary. Thankfully, the chocolate factory is no longer in the field of vision.

The stile brings you onto another lane. Turn right then immediately left over a stile into a field on the opposite side and cross this diagonally aiming towards an electricity pole in the middle to the left of some buildings. When you reach the fence line beyond it bear left and follow the fence around and, near the end of the field, cross a stile then a stone footbridge over a brook. After another stile you will exit onto a partially surfaced track with a lovely stone built farmhouse on the left. Go ahead on the track and, where it swings left after about 300 yards, cross a stile on your right into a field.

Stay with the hedged boundary towards the tree lined embankment ahead, which is in fact Offa's Dyke [2]. You go over a stile by a gate (beware, it can be very muddy here!) and you are immediately confronted with a crossing track with waymarks on a post opposite. Take the right option downhill following the line of the Dyke but after 100 yards or so cross a stile on your left into a field and walk uphill to exit via a stile/gate onto a junction of lanes.

Turn sharp right downhill following the acorn, the waymark symbol for Offa's Dyke, keep ahead at a crossroads after which the lane wiggles around a little and climbs. At the top of the rise cross a waymarked stile on your right into a undulating field, still on Offa's Dyke path, and follow the waymark direction through a broad gap in the right tree line. On emerging into a field bear half left diagonally across it to the lower right corner. Offa's Dyke should now be to your right and you negotiate a tall step stile over a stone wall then cross a waymarked stile into the adjacent field where you continue ahead with a hedge to your right. On reaching the end cross a tall waymarked stile in a dry stone wall onto Watling Street again.

Cross the road carefully turning right onto the footpath opposite and after a few yards turn off left down a waymarked track running alongside a property called 'Cloud Nine'. Ignore a gate opposite the house drive and continue up a green lane for 100 yards before going through a waymarked gate into a field and following the right boundary. The town of Trevor is prominent and you can see Wynnstay Hall (Lindisfarne College) on the hill to the right.

Cross a stile and turn immediately right at a waymark and then go over a fence stile to walk along the top of a field and through a crossing boundary, very slowly closing with the canal below. You can see a gate at the end and a stile to the right of it – cross this and turn left over the bridge, then immediately left again onto the towpath of the Llangollen branch of the Shropshire Union Canal.

You get glimpses of the Pontcysyllte Aqueduct ahead, but I have not yet got to that part of the story.

During the two years I worked on the Somerset House project I acquired much practical information and took this back to Scotland where I was to work on the refurbishment of Westerhall, a grand house close to my home. In this I was engaged by Sir William Pulteney, one of the richest men in the kingdom with considerable interests in Shropshire. A number of small building jobs followed but this was a fairly quiet time following a cut in public funds by the new Prime Minister, William Pitt the younger. Then came an invitation in 1784 to build a house in Portsmouth Dockyard for the resident commissioner.

I was at Portsmouth for two years. The hours were long and such spare time that I had was taken up by studying chemistry, writing poetry (badly) and corresponding with my friends back in Eskdale, particularly my boyhood companion, William Little. My next assignment came from Sir William Pulteney, who was now M.P. for Shrewsbury, and it was to make improvements to the castle there so that he could live in it while on business in the town. It seems as though I had a knack of arriving in the right place at the right time – opportunities unfolded and I took them. Certainly, the patronage of Sir William was in no small measure helpful to my advancement, but I think also that my appetite for hard work did not go unnoticed and I had acquired a little respect from my peers in the profession. Although I say so myself, I had a cheerful disposition and my broad Scottish accent seemed to endear me to people.

Anyway, I made a mark in Shrewsbury and I was asked to draw up plans for a new prison and then excavate the Roman town of Viriconium (Wroxeter) which is just outside the town. Further commissions followed in the form of planning the churches of St. Michael's, Madeley and St. Mary's, Bridgnorth, and it was while working on these projects that I was appointed the first ever County Surveyor for Shropshire. I do believe it possible that Sir

William was not without some influence in this. It was here that I discovered my real forte, building canals and bridges. One of my first jobs was to build a new bridge at Montford Bridge where the Holyhead Road crossed the River Severn. Then a new bridge at Buildwas, a short distance from the famous first Ironbridge which had been completed in 1779 (3).

The importance of canals was growing rapidly and in 1793 an Act of Parliament allowed the Ellesmere Canal Company to construct a network of canals to link the rivers Mersey, Dee and Severn. When I was asked to be the Chief Engineer I did not hesitate, I can tell you. The first section from Ellesmere Port to Chester presented few problems, the middle section from Chester through North Wales was abandoned because it was impossible to build. Instead I constructed the Horseshoe Falls at Llantysilio and guided the build-up of water into the canal which ran to Froncysyllte. It was here that I was faced with a major engineering problem – carrying the canal over the wide Dee valley.

Have you reached the aqueduct yet? Well, if not, please continue until you do, then read on.

The Pontcysyllte Aqueduct

Obviously time will not permit me to ramble on about all the events and personalities which led me to this point. They were many and I have both happy and sad memories of them. One thing I would mention, and you can still see it today – the Longdon aqueduct – a substantial structure made of iron to an entirely new principle at the time. An iron trough supported on three triangular piers set into masonry with a towing path slung on the outside. This was the model eventually adopted for Froncysyllte although, of course, the engineering considerations were on a totally different scale.

Just to give you some idea of the dimensions here, the aqueduct is 127 feet above the river, 1000ft long and is carried by eighteen stone piers embedded in sandstone rock. The trough is almost 12 feet wide and made of cast iron plates bolted together. It was completed in 1805 and the opening ceremony on 26th November was a spectacle to behold which received national coverage. A procession of barges crossed the aqueduct, there were field guns firing salutes, banners were displayed and there was patriotic music, all to the acclaim of 8,000 spectators who found such occasions to their taste so soon after Nelson's famous victory at Trafalgar. The completed structure was hailed as one of the 'wonders of Wales' and I hope that even now, at the dawn of the twenty-first century, it can be a little awe-inspiring.

At the same time as work was proceeding at Froncysyllte a second aqueduct got underway at Chirk, but you will see that a little later – after the tunnels!

If you feel in need of some refreshment at this juncture there is an alehouse on the other side of the aqueduct which bears my name, The Telford Arms. Otherwise or afterwards, about turn and walk back the same way and continue past the point of your earlier entrance onto the towpath along a quiet section of the canal.

Of course, I was involved with other projects. Work had started on plans for the Caledonian Canal which was to forge the last link in the series of waterways between the Atlantic and the North Sea through the Great Glen. This was to keep me occupied for all of the next twenty years and the engineering problems encountered followed by political criticism was nearly the death of me. Still, you don't want to hear too much about that as it is far removed from Shropshire. My other major work at the time was even further away – The Gotha Canal in Sweden which also took much longer than expected to complete. Canal mania was truly at its zenith at this time.

As you can see, my life was not spent in idleness! There was a perpetual round of problem solving, designing, advising etc., etc., and, oh!, the travelling! The travelling was dire indeed, so slow on horseback or by gig – if I had your motor cars how much more I could have achieved! You will understand me when I say that I had very little time for a social life, much less take a wife. My circle of friends was quite large, built up over many years through my profession, although I still retained my old friends, the most prominent of which were Andrew Little and Robert Southey. I like to think that I was esteemed and well liked, although I don't really know if that was the case. Perhaps your history books will shed light on that.

You go under another bridge and then through Whitehouse tunnel – 174 metres long. On the other side you pass Chirk Marina and the chocolate factory imposes itself again. Not for long, however, as you enter a cutting along another peaceful section before coming to another tunnel. This time it's the Chirk tunnel which is 421 metres long and, be careful, it is dark and uneven. Both tunnels were unusual in that they were built to a sufficient width to take a towpath. On most canals horses had to be led over the top while the boatmen 'legged it' along the tunnel walls. The cost was greater but this was more than compensated for by the increased speed of traffic. The far side brings you out onto the Chirk aqueduct over the Ceiriog Valley, again with spectacular views.

The railway viaduct was not, of course, there at the time the aqueduct was built. The design is more classical and, on this occasion, the iron trough was not used largely because Mr Myddleton, the owner of Chirk Castle, did not like it. To be fair, he had some reason to press his preferences bearing in mind the proximity of the structure to his estate and the fact that he was accommodating to our plans without demanding compensation.

Continue on the other side past Old Aqueduct Cottage and, on arrival at the next bridge, leave the canal by turning sharp left down a road in front of a post office. Walk along the right footpath past the 'Last Pub in England' (oops, sorry, what I said in the intro about the entire walk being in Wales was wrong – obviously we have slipped briefly into England here!) and on

The Chirk Aqueduct

A distant view of the Chirk Aqueduct

reaching a junction with the main road turn left along it. After the first road bridge turn right down a waymarked footpath alongside an antiques centre. Go over a fence and cross an old watercourse to continue along a path on the other side of it, after which take the right loop uphill. Exit via steps and a fence stile onto a road and turn right. Continue past a church and after 150 yards or so turn right back to the starting point.

The second part of my story deals with new challenges and the nightmare of Shelmore Bank, which was to be the death of me.

Notes:

1. Chirk Castle. A magnificent fourteenth century marcher fortress with elegant state rooms and beautiful mature parkland. Owned by the National Trust and open to the public. Tel: 01691 777701 for further details.

2. Offa's Dyke. Built in the late eighth century by the king of Mercia to define a frontier between his kingdom and the various Welsh kingdoms, and to control trade. Of the 81 miles of earthworks that can be traced today, 60 are contained within one unbroken stretch between Knighton and Chirk.

3. The old bridge at Buildwas was swept away during a violent storm in the winter of 1795.

Bibliography:

Lifelines, Rhoda M. Pearce, 1996

Thomas Telford, Anthony Burton, 1999

9

Thomas Telford – 2

1757 – 1834

Maps: Landranger 127; Explorer 242 & 243

Start: The Village Hall at Norbury, situated about five miles north-east of Newport off the A519. Please note that the start is at Norbury itself and not Norbury Junction, which is passed through on the walk. GR 783236

Walk Distance: 9½ miles, although it is possible to split into two separate walks by breaking off at Norbury Junction – see text.

Refreshments: The Junction Inn at Norbury Junction, The Boat Inn and The Navigation, both of which are on the canal at Gnosall.

Associated places of interest: Several mentioned in the text.

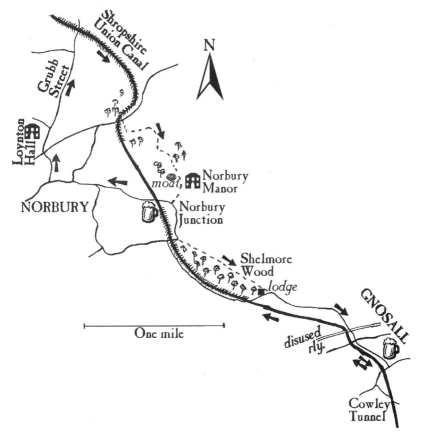

I don't want anyone to get the idea that the building of canals was my only forte. Although accepted as an expert in canal engineering my enthusiasm for other things, especially roads and bridges was not diminished. As I inferred in the first walk I could not do several things at the same time. Following completion of the Caledonian and Gotha Canals I was appointed by a Parliamentary Commission headed by Sir Henry Parnell as engineer for the construction of the London to Holyhead Road. This was in 1815, the year of our great victory at Waterloo. It was, perhaps, the largest single project I undertook and this involved the construction of numerous bridges, the most notable of which are at Conway and Betws-y-Coed. Indeed, the section through Snowdonia presented the severest test of my engineering skills as well as being the most impressive visually. The amount of rock that had to be blasted away to avoid problems of gradient or bends, was incredible and I was dubbed by my friend Southey 'The Colossus of Roads'!

Turn left out of Village Hall car park and, after a quarter of a mile, go straight ahead at crossroads signed Loynton and High Offley. You pass to the right of the Georgian Loynton Hall and into Grubb Street. After another half-mile you ignore a turning left after which the road descends gradually past some cottages to a bridge over the Shropshire Union Canal.

When I got to Bangor, an altogether new and challenging problem awaited – how to replace the slow and expensive ferry across the Menai Straits. The difficulties were immense with the tide running in different directions at great speed and there were constant violent winds coming down from the mountains. The result was a suspension bridge where sixteen great chains were attached to two massive stone piers on either side of the water. The first vehicle to pass along it was the London mail coach in January 1826. The Shrewsbury Chronicle at the time described the bridge as a 'stupendous structure' and some will regard it as the most significant of my achievements.

After this other jobs came along although my influence in road building began to decline. Construction of St. Katherine's Docks in London occupied much of my time and I began to get involved with a new mode of transport – the railways. It was this that led to my last major work. You see, the canal companies were very worried about the threat of railway competition and they countered this by work, under my direction, on the Trent & Mersey canal tunnels to improve the speed of passage. Then a movement begin in support of an entirely new canal and, following incorporation of the Birmingham and Liverpool Junction Canal Company in 1826, I was appointed its Chief Engineer.

When you reach the bridge divert left down the embankment before it and turn right to go under it onto the towpath. Notice the grooves cut deep into the posts through many years of ropes pulling narrow boats.

You go immediately into Grubb Street cutting which is one mile long and 90 feet high in places. Pass a mile post (Autherley Junction 17, Nantwich 22) and after about a mile go under bridge No.40. At the next bridge No. 39 [1] leave the canal about 100 yards before it via an embankment path and turn left across the bridge.

The idea was to carry the canal in the shortest possible distance between the Birmingham Canal and the Ellesmere and Chester Canal at Nantwich. There was also a branch from Norbury Junction to link with the Shrewsbury Canal so that coal and limestone could be transported to Birmingham and London more easily. All this required a number of large cuttings, embankments and tunnels to cope with the widely varying contours and ground conditions.

It was essential for the success of the project that the line was direct and with as few locks as possible. Of the twenty-nine locks on the whole length, all but four are grouped into flights at Tyrley, Adderley and Audlem just to the north of here. This meant a huge amount of cut and fill with embankments on a scale not hitherto attempted. This Grubb Street cutting is an example. By the summer of 1827 there were 1600 men working on the line.

Once you have crossed the bridge immediately bear right down a waymarked track. You shortly pass some trees on which is posted a notice stating this to be a permissive path.

The track loops left and twists and turns before passing to the right of a small wood. You come to a junction at the end of the wood and turn right onto a surfaced track (permissive as the actual definitive route goes across the adjacent field) which leads you round to a former moat by Norbury Manor. Continue past the Manor and ignore a waymark right before emerging onto a lane at Norbury Junction. We go left here but if refreshment is required turn right to the Junction Inn. It is from this point that you could cut short the walk and save the rest for another day. To do this simply bear left over the canal bridge at Norbury Junction and follow the lane (turning right at a junction) for a mile back into Norbury.

Having turned left onto the lane by Norbury Manor, stay on it until it swings sharp right towards a tunnel under the canal embankment (Shelmore Great Bank) and here go ahead on a broad waymarked bridleway along the back of Shelmore Wood. After 150 yards ignore a right turn to a fishery and continue ahead on a path bordering a field to the left of the wood. On reaching a junction with a concreted driveway to a house turn right to stay alongside the left edge of the wood. Eventually you exit by Shelmore Lodge onto a lane and turn left.

Remain on the lane as it goes under a bridge carrying a disused railway [2] into Gnosall. On reaching a junction with the A518 turn right, cross a bridge then turn left through a gate opposite the Navigation Inn down an embankment and onto the towpath ahead.

You walk through a marina and go under the next bridge, after a while passing the Boat Inn and onto the next bridge.

All along the line there were troubles. The original proposal was to excavate a 600 yard tunnel at Cowley through the solid sandstone rock. The rock was so unstable that most of the tunnel had to be opened up and in the end the tunnel was shortened to a much more modest 100 yards.

When you arrive at Cowley Tunnel, going through it is optional as we have to retrace our steps from this point. If you do go through please take care. When you emerge on the other side into a substantial cutting through the rock you will appreciate the scale of the project and the number of man-hours required to complete it. Continue back to the Navigation Inn and stay on the towpath for some distance, passing under the disused railway again then two more bridges before going over the road tunnel and on to Shelmore Embankment.

Cowley Tunnel

The problems at Cowley were nothing compared to the nightmare that was to follow at Shelmore. My preferred route for this section of the canal was through land owned by Lord Anson and he did not want it because it would interfere with his pheasant rearing and sport. Accordingly, the canal had to go in a curve round Shelmore Wood at considerable extra cost. How I cursed those pheasants I can tell you. Worse than that the embankment would not stabilize and was continually slipping away. There were 3-400 men working on this site and up to seventy horses bringing up the wagon loads of spoil. It was all very dispiriting and had an adverse effect on my health. In January 1833 I felt so wretched that I was unable to present my annual report to the committee.

With my agreement, a new man was brought in, William Cubitt. His idea was to lay much heavier material on top of the bank which would then sink down, forcing the poor material out to form a solid base. I did return briefly in 1833 to see how work on the Great Bank was progressing but I was now 77 years of age and felt it time to leave the work to others. I therefore resigned.

Poor Cubitt! The grand opening had to be postponed again because the bank was not ready. He reported to the committee the work 'has hitherto defied all our calculations as to the time of completion'. It did finally come to an end and was opened on 2 March 1835 but, unfortunately, I did not live to see it having died in September of the previous year ".

On arrival back at Norbury Junction leave the canal and turn left onto a lane and follow it back into Norbury.

It was my wish to be buried in the parish church at Westminster but the Institution of Civil Engineers had other ideas. Westminster, yes, but not the parish church – the Abbey. A signal honour indeed. I was not a rich man but did make a few bequests to old friends and enough to establish a library in Langholm, which is still there to this day.

Notes:

1. Called 'High Bridge'. Notice the telegraph pole on a platform at high level under the bridge – this is a survivor of the many lines which once existed on the canal banks.

2. The former Stafford to Wellington line built by the Shropshire Union Railway and Canal Company and opened in June 1849. It was closed for passengers in 1964 and completely in 1966.

3. From Telford's obituary notice in *The Shrewsbury Chronicle*:

> His gradual rise from the stonemasons and builders yard to the top of his profession in his own country, or we believe we may say, in the world, is to be ascribed not more to his genius, his consummate ability and preserving industry, than to his plain honest, straightforward dealing and the integrity and candour which marked his character throughout life.

Bibliography:

Lifelines, Rhoda M. Pearce, 1996

Thomas Telford, Anthony Burton, 1999

The
Infamous

10

Wild Edric

Second half of the eleventh century

Maps: Landranger 137; Explorer 201 and 216
Start: The car park by the castle and alongside the river in Clun,
South Shropshire. GR 298809
Walk Distance: 8¼ miles
Terrain: Generally easy going mainly on well used paths through
attractive countryside.
Refreshments: Plenty in Clun but none *en route*.
Associated place of interest: Clun Castle. Now a ruin and in the
care of English Heritage. Entry free at any reasonable time. See
Walk 11 in *Walks Through History* for more information on this
and other things of interest in Clun.

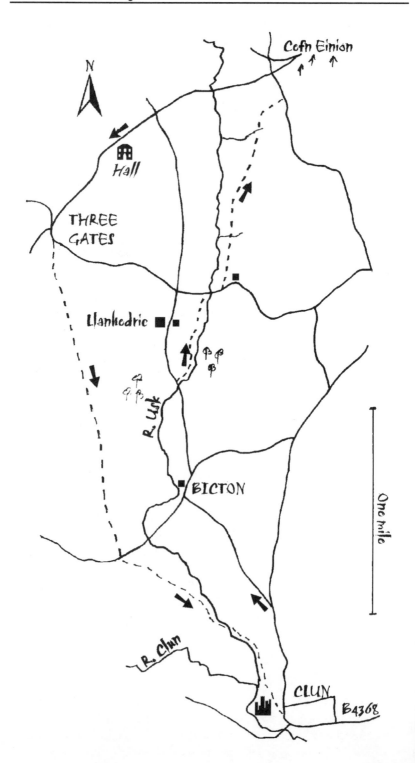

You know, I have to laugh. Was I real or was I not! Some say I am just a legend but let me tell you I was real all right. Can I help it if folks make up stories about me several hundred years after my death? Some of them I can scarce believe and I will tell you later – if I can stop from laughing that is. First though, I must say that if I were to speak in my eleventh century tongue you would hardly understand a word; therefore to make sense I am transforming it as best I can into your present dialect – just like one of my legendary feats really. Please bear in mind that I am a bit rough and ready and not your refined type of person such as you are used to!

Start from the Castle in Clun. It was just being built when I was around. By Robert de Say I think it was. Looks a bit different now though. Hardly surprising as it was burnt twice. Walk towards the town and turn left on the road towards Bishops Castle and Shrewsbury (A488 you call it). Pass the Buffalo Inn. Footpath runs out so be wary of moving things on wheels. How do you get them to go so fast? Yes, all right, I'm an ignorant savage but we had invented the wheel. Beware also when passing a farm as there is a blind bend after it. After a little over half a mile turn off left towards Bicton. You reach it after another mile.

I was a Saxon and a landowner before the Normans came, damn them. I had lands in Weston-under-Redcastle, Herefordshire and here in Clun so I was no peasant. I used to go hunting for boar and deer in the forests hereabouts. They were much bigger then than they are now. I mean the forests not the beasts, although they probably were too. Yes, you're all so prissy and civilized now – what would you do if suddenly faced with a savage wild boar, eh?

Anyway, the Normans came and took over my lands. As you can imagine I did not take kindly to this and refused to submit. One of my neighbours, yes one of my neighbours mind you – one Richard le Scrob from Richards Castle – was told to bring me into line. He'll have a job I thought and I rallied support from the Welsh kings who had fought with King Harold and some Cheshiremen. Together we stormed Hereford. I think the garrison there was so taken by surprise that they had no time to muster a fight and we beat them easily. The sight of all those Norman b......s lying with their guts spilling out was a mightily satisfying one for sure. They should have stayed in their own land.

Next we sacked Shrewsbury and laid siege to the Castle there which the Normans were still trying to build. Although this was not successful because of our inferior numbers and weapons, it worried William so much that he tried to make a truce with me.

Foolishly I went along with it hoping that I might make some gain. It seemed that everyone had come to terms with William except me and it was made clear that I could no longer hold out. I even helped him in a campaign against the Scots although some would say he only took me along so he could keep an eye on me.

As a reward I was allowed to live on my estates, much to the distaste of my followers. What happened after that is shrouded in mystery and that is how it is going to stay. I became something of a folk hero and many legends grew up around me. I will relate some of them to you in good time but, for now, you must accept that only I know the truth. I like hearing these stories although, as I say, they make me laugh and I don't wish to ruin the romance.

Go round to the right past Bicton Farm. Immediately after the farm turn left towards Three Gates and Mainstone. After another half mile or so you come to a bridge over the River Unk.

Some say I died in battle fighting against William near Stafford, because my truce with him did not last long. Others think I died in prison after capture and many simply say that I lived peacefully on my estates and died there of old age. You might prefer to believe that I did not die at all and am imprisoned in the lead mines on Stiperstones where I wait with my men and my wife, Godda. Why do I wait? It is because I allowed myself to be deceived by William the Conqueror and was thereby condemned to a fate of waiting to appear on the hills whenever the country is threatened.

One day in the middle of the nineteenth century, nearly 800 years after my 'death', a servant girl was walking the hills with her father when she heard the blast of a hunting horn. 'It's the wild hunt' her father said as my ghostly men galloped by with me, Wild Edric, at their head on a white horse with Godda beside me. Her long golden hair hung loose to her waist and in the white band around her head was an ornament of gold. 'Who are they?' asked the girl. 'We call them The Old Men,' said her father ' they have been imprisoned in the mines for hundreds of years. Miners say they can hear them knocking when working underground. Wherever the noise comes from they're sure to find the best lodes, but to see them riding is a bad sign'. A few months later the Crimean War broke out.

Those who believe this tale, and I'm not saying you shouldn't you understand, will also be interested to hear of our other appearances. Just before Napoleon's rise to power for example and at the time of the Boer War, World War I and the Falklands War. The Hundred Years War against the French was a good time too – we got out several times then!

Ignore a marker immediately before a bridge but take the second one about 50 yards after it, through a gate into a field.

Cross the field following the line of a stream on your right; go over a stile in the crossing boundary and another after a few yards to the right of a post and chain link fence. The river is still to your right but a little further away. Where the fence turns sharp left continue ahead for about 40 yards to the next stile. At this point 'Llanhedric' farmhouse can be seen over to the left. (Llan = church) This is the only surviving reminder of my name around here, apart from the footpath you will soon be walking on that is, and refers to an earlier building on the site. Cross a stile and follow the lower hedge along the line of the river to another stile. Cross the next field directly to cross a further stile on the far side onto a lane opposite a beautiful stone built cottage.

Turn right and cross the bridge over the river then turn immediately left at a marker between the cottage and outbuildings. You go through a gate then over a stile into a meadow where you veer half right to another stile in the top right corner. Cross the stile and a little stream after which you have to squiggle right then left to keep on the marked path and proceed alongside a post and wire fence to the next stile in a crossing boundary.

Cross that and walk along the bottom of the next field to cross another stile to the right of a group of trees. The mark directs you diagonally right across a field, your line gradually leaving the woodland boundary and aiming for a stile in the opposite hedge. You will find it just to the right of a pair of ash trees, about 100 yards up from the wood. Cross the stile and immediately negotiate a small brook then climb a shallow bank to emerge into the next field. Ignore a gate a few yards before the corner of this field and you will discover, hidden right in the corner, another stile.

Cross it and continue in the same direction, once again with the hedge on your left. At the end of this field, cross yet another stile to the left of a gate then immediately pass through a marked gate on your right and enter the adjacent field sloping up. Cross diagonally right upwards to the top left corner and after a stiffish climb cross a stile and turn half left, slicing off the bottom left corner of the next field. In the corner you will find a marker on a fence post but you don't go through. Instead go across the stream into the following field on an upward course with the hedge line on your right.

You climb up through an area of sparse trees, just after which you reach level ground and cross a stile on your right, bearing left then immediately right to follow the field boundary to cross yet another stile onto a lane to the right of a converted church. Well, I hope you managed to follow that all right – I would have just ridden over the land on horseback and stuff your silly rights of way. The land was probably mine anyway.

Turn left on a lane into the settlement of Cefn Einion. Turn left at the crossroads signed Threegates. There is a bit of a climb up to another crossroads where you go straight ahead and, after a further three-quarters of a mile turn left at yet another crossroads at Threegates.

As I have said, Godda was my wife. I will tell you how this came to be. One day me and my page got lost in Clun Forest. When night fell we were exhausted, trying to find our way and, at last, saw lights shining through trees. We came to a large manor house I had never seen before and I warned my page to be careful as it might be the work of witchcraft. 'We'll go nearer and see just what kind of people live here' he said. We could hear music playing and peeped into a room hung in rich tapestries and handsomely furnished. I stared in amazement. In the middle of the room was a group of ladies dancing in fine gowns and singing in a language I knew not. I was more than ever afraid this was the work of witchcraft and that if I went in I would be put under some deadly spell.

As I watched I noticed one of the young women, tall and slender and more beautiful than the rest. At once I fell in love and all fear of witchcraft vanished. I burst into the room and caught hold of the girl. At first the women were so startled that they carried on dancing. 'I want you for my wife' I told the girl. Then the dancing stopped and the others crowded round me, biting and scratching. They pulled and tugged and tried to rescue their sister but my page rushed into the room and between us we managed to carry her off into the forest.

At last I found my way back to my castle and ordered the very best food and wine to be brought. I begged the girl to forgive me for capturing her but she said nothing. Again I begged her to forgive me and told her that I would always love her. Still she said nothing. This continued for three long days then, at last, she spoke. 'I will be your wife Edric, and I will bring you happiness and good luck, but you must promise never to say one word against my sisters or my home. On the day that you do you will lose both me and your good fortune'.

I was overjoyed and readily made the promise. A magnificent wedding feast was set and noblemen from far and wide came to admire my beautiful wife. Even King William heard about her and asked to see her beauty for himself. I travelled to London and, at the moment William set eyes on Godda, he knew that everything he had heard about her was true.

For a long time I lived happily with Godda. I was kind to her and she gave me good fortune as she had promised. Then one night I came home from a hunting trip and Godda was nowhere to be found. I was tired and bad tempered and shouted out her name until she came to me. 'I suppose you've been to see those sisters of yours' I scowled. Before I could say another word, she vanished and it was then I remembered the warning she gave me before our wedding. For long weeks I searched the forest for her and tried to find the house where I had first seen her, but I never saw her again. It is said that I pined away and died [1] but that cannot be true if I am imprisoned in a mine with her, can it?

As the lane loops left after another 75 yards or so, go ahead through a gate onto a broad waymarked track. You are now on MY WAY, Wild Edric's Way – and the Shropshire Way.

Go through another gate still on a rising path, then another into an open field to follow a hedged boundary on the right towards a tree line ahead. Cross a stile in a crossing boundary and continue straight ahead across the middle of the next field towards the next stile which you can see in another tree line ahead. Cross this and in the top corner of the following field yet another and follow the top boundary of the next field to the right of a post and wire fence. Go over a stile in the crossing boundary from which down below to the half right you can see the village of Whitcott Keysett. As you approach the next stile, looking down to the left is Llanhedric Farm again.

Cross that stile, then two more in crossing boundaries before continuing ahead to the right of a line of hawthorn trees, ignoring a stile on the left. Cross the next stile, then three more at intervals after which you go down a short avenue of hawthorn trees around to yet another stile, following which you enter on a narrow path between sparse trees. At the bottom you come to a crossroads of ways. Ignore the orange marks and continue more or less ahead over a stile into a field and follow the top boundary of fence and trees.

Cross a stile by a gate, then stay ahead across an open field, with a good view of Clun Castle, pass two marker posts and, almost at the bottom of this field, hidden away under a hawthorn tree is a stile on your right which you cross into the adjacent field, walking to the left of a hedged boundary. Cross another stile onto a lane.

Go directly over the lane and another stile to continue on a marked trail. Cross a number of stiles with the River Unk below, then a footbridge and continue ahead in the next field aiming directly for the castle at first, but then keeping close to the river as it meanders along.

That's about it really. If you are walking over the South Shropshire Hills and see a man and a woman with long flowing hair at the head of some ghostly riders you should take immediate action and report the sighting to the authorities! Not that I was much for respecting authority of course, as I have told you. I may just appear again if England votes for the Euro and joins a federal state of Europe!

All this will not be given credence by those among you who believe that I haunt the hills in the form of a large black dog with fiery eyes. Usually at the scene of a murder or where a criminal has been gibbeted, where a suicide has been buried or where anybody has come to an untimely end.

I will leave you now to ponder and draw your own conclusions.

At the end of this field cross yet another stile, then another footbridge before going along a path between the river and hedge. The track turns hard and passes some cottages. Where it goes left go ahead across a stile into a field and after 20 yards go right through a gate and continue ahead to the right side of the boundary. This takes you to the left of the castle and you come out by a stile and turn left back into town.

Note:

1. Interestingly, this is recorded in a document written less than 100 years after his death.

Bibliography:
Witches & Warriors, Shropshire Books, Karen Lowe, 1990
Shropshire Folklore (updated from original 1883 edition by Charlotte Burne), Georgina Jackson

11

Bloody Jeffreys – The Hanging Judge

1645 –1689

Maps: Landranger 126; Explorer 241
Start/Park: Car park in centre of Wem, North Shropshire, by large supermarket.
Walk Distance: 5 miles or 6 miles
Terrain: Fields and lanes in a quiet corner of the county
Refreshments: Plenty in Wem, none *en route*

First of all, please excuse my direct manner; I was never one to say two words when one would do – I was a judge after all although the same may not be said about some of my modern contemporaries. Never was a man so unjustly reviled as I, George Jeffreys, Lord Chancellor of England. They called me 'Bloody Jeffreys' the Hanging Judge merely on account of doing my duty by God and the King.

From the carriage park go to the High street and turn left then right alongside the Castle Inn on a public footway. Go across a lane and past the end of some gardens before arriving at another main road. Cross this almost directly up Wemsbrook Road. When reaching the end take the signed public footpath to Lowe Hill. After 50 yards you come to a junction with another residential road and turn right then take the second on the right into Meadow Close. Immediately enter the footpath alongside No.54 which takes you over a stile into a field. I just can't get over how the town has expanded since my day and I must say I do not altogether like it. Never mind, times move on.

Keep to the left boundary and at the end cross a waymarked stile and continue the line ahead in the next field. The boundary wiggles in and out a

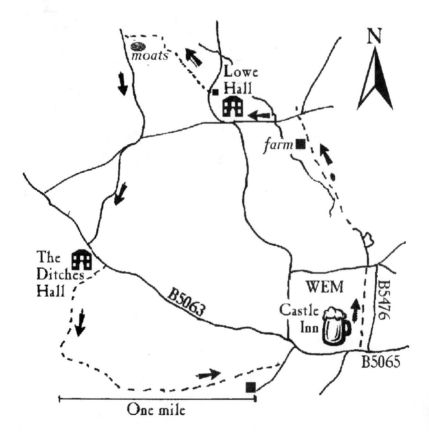

One mile

bit with the line of a brook. You skirt round the edge of a pool and continue on the other side where the ground is a bit rough and uneven to a gate in the far boundary with a farm in view. Cross a fence stile by the gate, then follow the waymark to the half right bisecting the field heading towards barns to the right of a house. In a short distance join a hedge boundary on your left going directly towards the barns.

Keep to the right of the barns and go through the left hand of two gates to enter the farmyard on a concrete surface. Bear left in front of the first barn then immediately right to exit the complex along a broad stony track that eventually leads you out into a lane. Turn left on the lane and after a quarter of a mile arrive at the settlement of Lowe. Right on the corner there is Lowe Hall, my country house in the late seventeenth century. Indeed I held the manors of Wem and Loppington at that time, having purchased them from one Daniel Wycherley of Clive. Due to the fire in 1677 and bankruptcy he was forced to sell his lands to me in order to clear his debts. At least he kept his head!

Lowe Hall

Yes, Duty, I said! The traitors (supporters of Monmouth's rebellion against my sovereign James II, you understand) deserved nothing less I tell you nor did most of the other sycophants, plotters and profligates I dispatched to the Almighty. What was a man in my position supposed to do? Give them a slap and ask them to kindly behave better in future? No! Any sign of weakness would be seized upon by my enemies as an opportunity to challenge my authority and fitness for office.

On 6 February 1685 King Charles the Second died and was succeeded by his brother James, by which time I had risen to the high office of Lord Chief Justice of England. As you probably know, Charles had no legitimate heir but he had a number of illegitimate offspring (as many of us did!) including the Duke of Monmouth, who had been banished from Court for being implicated in the Rye House Plot[1] two years earlier. Also, at around this time I was made a peer and took the title of Baron Jeffreys of Wem.

Now, as you may know, Monmouth rebelled against the Catholic James and assembled a rabble of an army in the West Country which was soon defeated by the King's forces at Sedgemoor, two miles from Bridgwater, on 6th July 1685. It happened that the Western Circuit Assizes was part of my remit and I descended under military escort on Dorchester to dispense the King's justice. There were around 300 prisoners awaiting trial there and nearly 1500 at four other Assize courts in the region – far too many to deal with in the allotted time of three weeks. If only a quarter of them chose to plead not guilty their cases could drag on for months and the entire legal calendar disrupted as a result.

Pollexfen, my Chief Prosecutor, and I agreed on what can best be described as a seventeenth century version of what you would call 'Catch 22'. The prisoners were informed that if they pleaded guilty they might escape execution but, if they pleaded not guilty and were subsequently convicted, they would be executed with the minimum delay. Clever what? As a result most pleaded guilty and, on the first day, of the thirty pleading not guilty, only one was acquitted. Only thirteen of the remainder were executed because the sheer physical task of hanging and quartering so many was simply beyond Ketch[2]. Their heads and quarters were hanged upon poles in the town.

Of those who pleaded guilty, 251 received sentence of death, of whom sixty-two were executed – in various other places. We moved on to Taunton, the hotbed of rebellion, where 500 awaited the State's retribution at an Assize lasting a mere two days. All but a handful disputed their guilt and these, together with 139 of the remainder were ordered for execution. Others were deported as servants for £10 or £15 apiece. The whole business occupied nine days of my time, during which time over 1700 rebels were dealt with, about 800 ordered for deportation and 300 receiving death *sentences, their body parts being scattered around the West Country in gruesome fashion. Such is the price of treason.*

Have you had a look at my house yet? It is now an hotel and you can stay there if you dare[3] The crest on the front incidentally, is not mine but that of the Barnes family who lived there before me.

When ready to continue turn right at the junction (i.e. towards Whixall). Alternatively, if you wish to cut the walk short by about a mile, go ahead and after about a third of a mile you will meet a lane coming in from the right – now continue from ★ below (except that you will turn *left* towards Loppington). If not taking this option, after another 250 yards or so you reach Lowe Villa and, just past it, take the waymarked stile on your left into a field. Turn half right to meet the right boundary and follow that along.

Cross a stile at the end, which may have barbed wire across, walk along the short boundary of the next field and cross two stiles with a footbridge between and into the next field. Take extra care here as the first stile was broken and the footbridge slippery[*]. Continue the same line adjacent to the right boundary. At the end cross a stile and bear immediately left along the post & wire boundary you have just crossed. As the boundary changes to hedge, look across to your left for a succession of depressions behind the houses. These are the 'moats' referred to on your survey maps. Keep going with the boundary over rough ground until exiting via a stile by a gate onto a lane. Turn left on the lane through an agricultural settlement and after a pleasant walk of just over half a mile you reach a junction where you could have cut short from Lowe.

★ *I suppose you could say that I was a man of contradictions. Well before the Bloody Assizes my notoriety as the most feared judge in the land (arrogant and hated many would say) was established yet this upholder of justice was hard-drinking and loud-mouthed when not so pre-occupied. A figure of high gravity and authority by day, a drunken roisterer by night. Little did my critics know that it was the increasing agony of a stone in the bladder which drove me to excess and, to not a small degree, contributed to my brutality in court. Did I not say that I was unjustly reviled? I had not the time for medics, let alone a risky operation, but eventually paid for this arrogance with my life.*

I was a fanatical Tory yet consorted with Whigs when it suited my purpose. Mark you, I did for quite a few of them in court. Those implicated in the Rye House Plot were Whigs, of course,

[*]   Both matters reported to the local Rights of Way Officer and, hopefully, will be remedied.

and they rightly suffered the full venom of my explosive outbursts when they were brought before me. In general the Whigs were odious and a threat to the monarchy and I took every possible opportunity to reduce their influence (and numbers).

I was a devout supporter of the Church of England yet loyal to the Catholic James II. The political machinations of the day were, as ever, complicated by religious considerations but it was my earnest endeavour to deal evenly with all regardless of their faith. I hope you believe that even though many literary works and commentaries would have you think otherwise.

Turn right towards Loppington but, after you round the bend take the first left turn along a narrow little used lane, unsuitable for motor vehicles. Keep on the lane ignoring a waymark left after a while . Eventually you can see the Long Mynd in the distance with The Lawley and Caer Caradoc in front of it. Further to the right is Breiddon Hill surmounted by Rodney's Pillar[(4)]. On reaching the B5063 turn left – be careful there is no footpath. You pass the splendid Ditches Hall on the right and, shortly afterwards halfway round an S bend, turn off right on a public footpath signed the Ditches Farm.

Following his defeat Monmouth pathetically pleaded to King James for his life. The King demanded to know how he could expect to be pardoned when his Declaration had branded him (the King) a murderer of Charles II. Monmouth debased himself by crawling to embrace the King's knees and weepingly replied `Ferguson drew it and made me sign it before I ever read it.' Small wonder the King turned away angrily and told him to prepare to die. He was executed two days later by Ketch who was grossly overpaid for the most botched job in many a long year. After three blows, with the prisoner still alive, Ketch hurled away the axe saying `God damn me, I can do no more.' The crowd threatened to kill him if he did not finish the job and he was forced to take out a great knife to sever the head completely. Well on towards Christmas 1685, rebels were still being executed and people had become sickened. In the spring of 1686 the lumps of human flesh scattered around the West Country started to stink abominably and James himself issued orders for the gruesome relics to be removed. Oh, sorry – I do hope you are not too squeamish.

Soon after these events I was appointed Lord Chancellor – at the age of 40 the youngest man ever to have held the post. I must say that what I found was most disturbing. Delays of inordinate length in bringing cases to trial, lazy and corrupt officials and incompetent lawyers charging exorbitant fees. A firm grip was required to rectify this state of affairs and soon a number of officials were ousted and even some imprisoned. The whole system became much improved (there, I told you I wasn't all bad!) but I made enemies amongst those who had lived well under the old system. My health deteriorated due to the damned bladder stone and drink, a habit which increased because of the stress involved with my new and eminent post. Lavish entertaining depleted my funds and rumours spread that my days in office were numbered.

I always knew that religion would come to the fore again and so it proved. I found it increasingly difficult to maintain both my fervent Anglican faith and my influence in a Catholic Court. My favour with the King gradually diminished as the King sought to advance his Catholic friends throughout the establishment and overcame all obstacles to this endeavour[5]. The King became ever more headstrong and his policies ill thought out – to the extent that I became increasingly isolated. Eventually I was the only great officer of state who supported the Church of England.

The mounting attacks on the Church of England were unpopular with the people who refused to suffer the subversion of their laws and religion. Intrigue was rife with several eminent persons secretly courting William of Orange. Not I you understand; as the French ambassador reported 'The Chancellor, a very violent man, is the only one who is not involved in intrigue.' The King was now hell-bent on disaster and nothing I could do would save him and, to be honest, I felt less and less like doing so anyway due my continued bad health. By re-issuing the Declaration of Indulgence, commanding that it be read in every church in the country, and by insisting that Parliament would have to contain a majority of Catholics, James brought the nation to the edge of rebellion.

Nice views open up here. You pass the entrance to the farm after which the path twists and continues on the other side of the boundary hedge. Go to the left of derelict farm buildings and continue on the track as it swings sharp left to the right of a hedge field boundary. The track now turns right across the field but you continue ahead keeping close to the hedge line. Walk along to where there is a little kink in the boundary and turn off half-right across the bottom left corner of the field to find a double stile with a footbridge on the adjacent boundary about 150 yards up from the corner. Cross the footbridge into the next large field and turn right with a mixed tree boundary on the right and after about 100 yards, at a point where the boundary swings sharp right and well before reaching the end of the field, cut left across the field passing under a lone oak to a stile you can see beyond in the fence line in front of a line of bushes.

In fact it is another double stile with a footbridge and you cross into the next field where you continue ahead alongside the mixed tree boundary. The chimney stack ahead belongs to 'Wem Mills', a disused and apparently preserved animal feed mill on the Shrewsbury Road out of town. At the end cross a stile into another field and continue adjacent to the right boundary. Cross yet another stile and follow the left hedged boundary to cross another stile with farm buildings in view on other side of the next field. Cross another stile then another before bearing half-right to the last stile on the adjacent boundary onto a track between houses. Turn left to exit onto the main street and turn right back to the starting point.

The prospect of a Dutch invasion came ever more likely as my efforts to persuade James to more moderate policies were thwarted. He did at one point see some sense and put in train conciliatory measures but these were in vain. The Prince landed at Torbay on 5th November 1688 and James hastened to Salisbury to marshal his army. He returned to London after a week but not before some of his supporters had defected to the enemy. Feckless cowards who turned coat to protect their heads! Things went from bad to worse as desertions took place daily and there were uprisings throughout the land. On 11th December James admitted defeat and fled secretly to France. With this I was sorely aggrieved. Why, after all my years of loyal service did he not take me into his confidence? Even worse, he deliberately deceived me by ordering me to report to the royal closet the morning after he planned to flee!

As the news of the King's flight spread the mob in London exacted revenge on anything Catholic and anybody connected to King James. I was captured at Wapping the day after and carried a dishevelled wreck through baying crowds to the Lord Mayor. I was then escorted to the Tower of London – the only place I could feel safe at that time. The widows of Monmouth's rebels demanded my execution but it was not granted. My illness gave them what they sought. Physical agony increased daily as diseased kidneys became the inevitable consequence of the bladder stone and death came on 19th April 1689, a few weeks short of my 44th birthday. Ironically, I was buried in the tower chapel close by Monmouth.[6]

Notes:

1. The Rye House Plot – an attempt to assassinate Charles II and the Duke of York by an ambush on the road to London. It was thwarted by a fire at Newmarket which caused the King to return to London earlier than

expected. The main perpetrators William Russell and Algernon Sydney were condemned to death by Jeffreys.

2. Jack Ketch, executioner. His assistant Pascha Rose was by trade the bloodily appropriate one of butcher.

3. Lowe Hall Farm – Bed & Breakfast available. Stay the night in Bloody Jeffreys' house! Tel: 01939 232236

4. Rodneys Pillar. On the summit of Breiddon Hill and erected in 1781 to commemorate Admiral Lord Rodney's naval victories over the French.

5. Principally the Test Act, which imposed on office-holders the duty of worship according to the rites of the Church of England, and by manipulation of The Ecclesiastical Commission.

6. Four years later his family were allowed to transfer his remains to St. Mary, Aldermanbury. The church was bombed during the winter of 1940/1 and all traces of the coffin were lost.

Bibliography

Bloody Jeffreys, The Hanging Judge, Milne-Tyte, Robert, 1989

12

Mad Jack Mytton – 1

1796 – 1834

Maps: Landranger 126; Explorer 240
Start: Car park by Whittington Castle (courtesy fee – 50p for upkeep of Castle, now privately owned). The village is situated at the crossroads of the A495 and the B5009, two miles north-east of Oswestry and about 5 miles south-west of Ellesmere.
Walk Distance: 6½ miles
Terrain: Generally easy going across fields, along lanes and a canal towpath.
Refreshments: In Whittington or the Jack Mytton Inn *en route*.
Associated place of interest: Whittington Castle – Now a rather sad ruin but it has a long and violent history. It was built in the twelfth century by Roger de Montgomery and passed to the Peverels before coming into the hands of the Fulke Fitzwarines. It was the scene of local battles for supremacy between neighbouring families and there are tales of betrayal, murder and suicide. Fulke II fell out with King John over the grant of lands and was cast out as an outlaw. The king pursued him up and down the country with 100 men and legends abound of his adventures. He was a sort of Robin Hood character and, indeed, there is some evidence that he was Robin Hood. In 1215 he joined the baronial revolt which led to the signing of Magna Carta. A little research will provide a fascinating insight into the history of the castle and its inhabitants. Also, see footnote [1].

Rake, drunkard, womaniser, inveterate gambler and brute – I have been called the lot and more besides. I am not proud of the life I led and perhaps it was a mercy to everyone that it was cut short. Sakes knows what fiendish exploits I would have got up to had I lived longer. My only consolation is that I did give great entertainment to some of those to whom my antics did not cause direct harm and, at the end, forgiveness seemed to prevail almost everywhere.

Return to the mobile tin box park entrance, cross the road and turn right opposite the church and walk along the Shrewsbury Road (B5009). Unfortunately it is necessary to continue along here for about three-quarters of a mile (sorry about that. No – I'm not a bit sorry really, ha ha! You people built it, and the dratted mobile tin box, so you can jolly well walk along it. In my day it was just a quiet country lane). After you

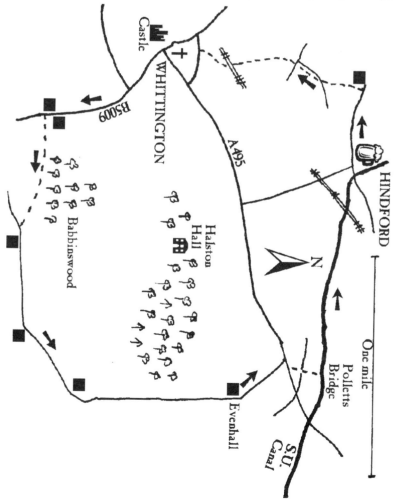

Whittington Castle

pass the entrance to Alder Lea on your left and about 100 yards further on cross a stile into a field. Walk over the field directly and go over another stile on the opposite side before bearing half right through the next field. Go through a gap in the next crossing boundary to a fence stile taking you along the right edge of Babbinswood[1].

Cross the next stile, then move away from the wood/field edge by walking across an open section of field keeping the wood about 50 yards to your left aiming to the right of some cottages you can see beyond the next field. If the field is planted you may wish to consider walking around the edge (that is to say, staying with the wood boundary). You should find a stile in a crossing boundary about 50 yards in from the left corner and if it is obstructed by a hedge, don't blame me! Get over this and cross the next field directly to exit via another stile alongside a gate onto a lane where you turn left. Again, if this last field is cropped then, oh dear, you may have little choice but to pick your way across it.

Maybe I should send my horse Baronet and a gig to help you across. But then again, with my reputation for practical jokes you may not think that a good idea. I remember once taking a passenger in my gig – some local horse dealer. I can't recall now who it was but I didn't care for him – and I urged my steed on to an ever more frantic pace. I asked the man whether he had ever been upset in a gig. Fortunately, no he said, to which I replied 'Well you have now!' and swerved towards a bank and hoisted the nearside wheel to a sharp angle up the incline. Over went the gig and we were both flung to the ground. What fun!

You walk along this pleasant lane for some time – for about 1½ miles in fact – passing a number of farms and cottages some of which are old enough for me to remember. The wood on the left which you pass after about a mile obscures Halston Hall where I was born in September 1796 and where I lived much of my life. If you can't see it through the trees, don't worry – we will get other chances later.

My father, bless him, was a landed gent of high respectability and lived well with about 40 servants and workers on the accumulated wealth of several generations. I will tell you how I managed to lose it all in just a few years.

A mere two years after my birth my father died and I became heir to all his estates and income, but it was a blow which affected me deeply. My mother, Harriet, was a quiet woman who was quite incapable of bringing me up in the way my father would have wanted, that is, schooled in the country pursuits of hunting and shooting. Consequently, I was allowed to run wild and unchecked, strutting around the farmyard like a young gamecock and being given anything I wanted. No one dared to lay a finger on me and I grew totally undisciplined. However, what I lacked in discipline I gained in knowledge of the land and a great affinity with animals. I had no fear of them and they followed me around as though bewitched – even the fiercest hound would take from my hand, much to the amazement of my attendants. In my last days, when everything had turned to dust, I looked back on those times with fond memories and not a little regret.

My knack with animals enabled me to become involved with husbandry at a very early age, encouraged by the men on the estate who, though I say so myself, admired my spirit. I was so full of pranks and practical jokes that one of our neighbours nicknamed me 'Mango, the King of the Pickles'. A name that I was destined to live up to until my life's end.

I began to spend a lot of my time among the ostlers and stable hands, acquiring a great deal of knowledge and some rich language! I couldn't have given a fig for most of the superficial 'friends' my mother invited to the house; in fact I despised them all and the cloying patronage of their husbands. No, horses and dogs were much more interesting and I began to become restless and even more untamable. In despair, my mother asked the new curate of Whittington, the Rev. William Wynne Owen to undertake the onerous task of bringing me to heel.

It was a baptism of fire for Mr. Owen alright! My first practical joke was to put a black pony in his bedroom from which it refused to budge having taken an inexplicable fancy to the man. It then followed him around like a pet dog. Even so, he was a shrewd man and through his great knowledge of the Stud Book gained my confidence and I began to confide in him as I might have done to my father.

I became obsessed with hunting and determined to become one of the country's leading exponents of the sport. Thankfully, I was well liked in the neighbourhood and the passage of my hounds was usually tolerated without grudge. To be sure, I had to settle a few compensation claims but this underpinned my popularity even if it became a drain on my finances. By early 1807 I was running my own pack, the spectacle of which caused great hilarity amongst the Halston villagers I do recall. I was only ten after all though almost totally independent of my mother and ever closer to Mr. Owen.

All this was to end with a jolt in June 1807 when I was sent to Westminster School. No amount of tantrum on my part would deflect my mother from this course but the journey south on the mail coach was so absorbing that, by the time I reached London, I had almost forgotten Halston and was looking forward eagerly to new adventures.

Can you just glimpse the house over to the left as the lane swings around Evenall Farm? Well, no matter, when you eventually reach a junction with the A495 turn right and cross onto a grass verge opposite. After about 100 yards go left over a double stile and follow the left edge of a field and, at the end of it, cross a beam bridge. Do try not to fall off, though I would laugh heartily if you did. Continue the line forward across the next field then, after some 80 yards, bear left through a gap in the boundary and continue the line forward in the adjacent field but to the left of the same boundary. There is an area of marshy ground to cross which hopefully will present you with huge difficulty and you then go over a stile in front of Pollett's Bridge before bearing right and then going round to the left and under it onto the towpath of the Shropshire Union Canal (Llangollen Branch). For your education, this is a 'Roving Bridge' which enables horses drawing boats to change towpath sides without having to uncouple.

100 yards after the next bridge but one, No.8, if you look over to your left you can just see the upper storeys and roof of Halston Hall – not much of a view I know but be patient. Now, more education! The bridge, No. 9, is very unusual in having a wooden deck supported by curved beams instead of the usual brick arch. You stay on the towpath until arriving at the Jack Mytton Inn after bridge No. 11.

Public Schools were tough places but I was quick with my wit and my fists so was soon accepted as a sportsman. Cock-fighting was a favourite pastime but landed me in deep financial trouble through heavy betting losses. I played hard and studied little but came away a man. Indeed, I came away sooner than expected – you see I was expelled for unacceptable behaviour, which is a polite way of putting it. I was still only fifteen and was sent to Harrow to complete my education. This episode was short lived. During three terms I fought eight pitched battles, after which I was again required to remove myself. The black sheep returned to Halston once more.

I was a little more learned but had also learned to drink! The pleasures of alcohol took such a hold on my persona that it was tantamount to slow poisoning. Drinking was, of course, a social obligation in these times and to hell with obesity and gout! Only wimps were incapable of downing a bottle of port after dinner. Mr Owen tried to persuade me to enter university. 'I'll see you damned first' I said but he won in the end and I went to Cambridge.

While all this was happening the country was at war with France, as even those with a modicum of historical knowledge will know. Bonaparte had been routed by the Russians during his ill fated invasion of 1812 and subsequently abdicated two years later. The end of the war spelt the end of the university scheme so I was free again and set off for Paris. I came back a year later even wilder and completely broke. Trouble was that I was always a soft touch where money was concerned and opportunities to, what do you say – rip me off – were plentiful.

The drinking bouts resumed and so did the riotous parties with my sporting friends. The estates were left to my agents who were honest men who somehow managed to keep things going. A few dalliances with Shrewsbury tavern girls furthered my growing reputation as a rake but, throughout, I acted honourably and also tried to look after the welfare of my tenants, as indeed a gentleman of breeding should. There were still three years to go before I could claim my inheritance and time seemed to stretch into eternity, punctuated only by the excitement of Wellington's victory at Waterloo. The amount of money I was spending on sport was, I admit, reckless as indeed was my over generous largesse to the poor. I was obliged to sell a few pictures when times got hard. My escapades bore the hallmark of complete irresponsibility, though it did not seem that way to me at the time, *and my mother and Mr. Owen determined that a change of scene was necessary.*

There is a gateway access through the car park to the Jack Mytton Inn. Fancy that now – they've named an alehouse after me! Never did I think I would attain such status. Inside there is some information about me, if you're interested. On leaving go onto the lane and turn right then right again at a junction. Continue past some houses and a large isolated house on the left. About 200 yards further on and before a farmhouse go left over a stile.

My admiration for the war heroes led me to purchase a commission in the 7th Hussars. Cornet Mytton I was and proceeded forthwith to London. Soon I was larking about with others of my kidney and again lost heavily at gambling. It was during a stint in France that I purchased my beloved Baronet who served me well throughout my time in the army. He only had one eye you know. On my return to Halston he proved to be a superb hunter.

The next major episode in my life was marriage! Who on earth would want to tie themselves up to a dissolute waster like me? Harriet Emma, daughter of the late Sir Tyrwhitt Jones of Stanley Hall did – I was after all a country Squire and perhaps she thought herself able to cure me of my profligate ways. Oh, I almost forgot, before that I came of age. Halston had not seen a like celebration since the day I was born. It was ablaze with lights; even the Whittington Road was lit up with lanterns. There was a firework display, dancing and food and drink a plenty.

I promised Harriet Emma everything. I truly loved her but she became clinging and given to silly chatter so I went back to Shrewsbury and to drink. One day I took her to visit the hounds and shut her in with them so that their muddy paws and wet tongues ruined her gown. I whooped in delight at her screams and, when eventually released, she went off to complain to my mother. The story got out into all the great houses and became corrupted so that it seemed I had set the hounds on my wife and hunted her all over the estate. What a brute! they exclaimed.

My entry into the world of horse racing was unsuccessful but it did bring me into contact with Charles Apperley who was rather more successful in undoing all that my wife had done in persuading me towards a more sober life. Over indulgence turned to alcoholism which blinded me to my wife's delicate state of health. She was also with child and produced me a daughter, to my great disappointment. 'I'll have it smothered' I declared though not really meaning it and soon began to take an interest in the little creature. My wife, however, remained in poor health with consumption from which she would never recover. I went off to attend to other affairs – the vacant parliamentary seat of Shrewsbury no less for which I was to stand as a Tory candidate.

Keep to right boundary in the field, go through a gate in a crossing boundary then cross a stile on your right and follow the fence line around to a footbridge. Once over the footbridge cross the next field roughly on the same line heading for the end of a line of trees where there is another footbridge to cross.

Cross the next field to a stile on the opposite boundary about 150 yards ahead and where you might encounter a little more marshy ground. Once in next field bear half right to meet the boundary and continue uphill with it round the edge of a small spinney and to the top corner where you go through a gate. In the adjacent field keep to the right of the hedged boundary and at the end cross a stile onto a track between fence and hedge. You cross another track and bear round to the right onto what is a section of dismantled railway[2] which was not even built in my time. After about 100 yards look for some steps on your left up to a stile.

Cross the stile and turn right in a field to another stile in the adjacent boundary 120 yards ahead, cross that and continue the same line across the next field passing between two oaks to the top far corner by a cemetery. Go through a wicket gate onto a tarmac driveway between houses and on reaching the road in Whittington turn right then left at a junction back to the start. The promised better view of Halston Hall? Oh yes, there isn't one! You can't get near it. Just my little joke…I was renowned for them after all. [3]

Notes:

1. Whittington Castle is reputedly the scene from which the Babes were taken to be left to die in the Wood – Babbinswood – by their wicked uncle in order to gain their inheritance. However, there are numerous variations on this story and just as many reputed locations for it, although Norfolk is another strong contender. It has been popularized in comedy and pantomime when even Robin Hood has been drawn into the plot.

2. Formerly part of the Great Western Railway, closed in 1965.

3.Halston Hall is not open to the public and there are no access rights on the estate.

Bibliography:
The Life and Times of Squire John Mytton of Halston, Holdsworth, Jean, 1972
Tales of Old Shropshire, Lawrence-Smith, Kathleen, 1991

13

Mad Jack Mytton – 2

1796 – 1834

Maps: Landranger 137; Explorer 217
Start: Any convenient place in Church Stretton, which is on the A49 Shrewsbury-Leominster Road.
Walk Distance: 7 miles
Terrain: Very mixed – quiet lane and pretty villages but a little gentle climbing is required here and there in superb countryside.
Refreshments: Plenty in Church Stretton but none on the route.
Associated place of interest: Chillington Hall, Nr. Brewood, South Staffordshire. Home of the Giffard family and source of Mytton's second wife. The Hall is open to the public from 2-5pm on Easter and both May Bank Holiday Sundays, Thursdays in July and Thursdays, Fridays and Sundays in August.

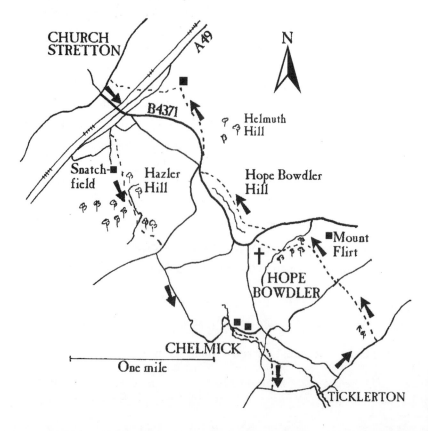

If you thought the first walk showed me up for the blackguard I was, wait until you read this! Surely I was the most miserable wretch ever to have walked the fair county of Shropshire. First though, a few directions.

You first of all need to go out eastwards along the main street to its junction with the A49 and cross it directly into Sandford Avenue, which is the B4371 Bridgnorth Road. After a few yards take the first turning on the right down Watling Street South then take the second left alongside Sandford Court Nursing Home followed by an immediate left turn at the rear of it into Snatchfields Lane. You go almost immediately right again along a public bridleway with the Jack Mytton Way marker. YES, a footpath named after me, what a laugh! My infamy still recalled nearly two centuries later – I can't believe it. [1] The broad track weaves between some 'modern' houses and emerges to cross a hammerhead to continue between a wall and a hedge heading towards Hazler Hill with its strange structure on top used by you people to communicate. What a blot on the landscape!

You realise, of course, I am talking to you in your own terminology – none of this was here in my time, thank God. How do all you people manage to live together cheek by jowl in these little brick boxes without so much as space for exercising a horse? On second thoughts I could have had an incredibly good time causing chaos with all your hi-tech equipment – it would undoubtedly have become an obsession with me to be the world's most feared planter of computer viruses. The result would have been the same though as in my real life – arrest and imprisonment.

Go through a gate into a paddock then through two more gates before and after Snatchfield Farm to enter a pasture field keeping to right of the boundary fence. After about 100 yards the fence turns 90 degrees right but here continue half left up the grassy slope on a just about discernable path towards the trees ahead. The track broadens as it goes through the trees where you pass through a gate to stay ahead, immediately crossing a small brook. Follow it upwards but only for a short while until the path rises above and turns away from it.

Go through another gate and continue on a narrow, hedged path to pass a small redundant quarry on your left before exiting onto a lane. Ragleth Hill is over to your right now. Do not enter the public footpath opposite but turn right on the lane and after about 250 yards at the first junction turn left towards Chelmick. You can see the outline of Wenlock Edge ahead with the top of the Wrekin behind it, and Hope Bowdler Hill soon becomes visible to your left. Keep on this lane until you reach Chelmick Farm and other buildings in the hamlet.

If you remember, at the end of part 1, my wife was very ill and I was about to stand for Parliament. Well, to the surprise of many, I was elected. Perhaps it was due to a combination of my speeches, during which I profusely apologized for the follies of my youth, and my unique method of canvassing. You certainly needed a long pocket to 'buy' votes in those days and I developed the idea of riding around Shrewsbury wearing a coat with gold buttons and a ten pound note attached to each for the voters to snatch at. My family, poor souls, thought that the time had come at last for the end of my wild days but, alas in that they were sadly mistaken. The stuffy, boring and patronizing atmosphere of the Commons was insufferable and within half an hour I left for Shropshire never to be seen in Westminster again!

I spent more time drunk than sober now and the events of the outside world simply passed me by, including the furore of discontent by the poor against the harshness of their conditions. I still hunted and spent thousands of pounds on it, mainly with the Albrighton, and got up to some high jinks I can tell you. There was the time when, having soaked myself falling into a brook, I went home draped in a red flannel petticoat worn by the women of these parts. You should have seen the look on their faces at Halston! Then there was the time when I plunged into a lake on horseback in order to win a bet on who would be first back. And the dinners, oh the dinners! They were such exuberant affairs where the wine flowed well into the night along with a never-ending string of absurd antics. My pet bear was a popular treat – I would come in riding her around the table until she growled savagely. Some guests were clearly terrified of the creature, much to my mirth of course.

Sadly, my contempt for Parliament and neglect of my wife rankled with the county squirearchy and this was exemplified by the death of Harriet Emma in July 1820. I was beside myself with grief and self-reproach and, after the period of

Jack Mytton on his pet bear

mourning, threw myself again into the Hunt. Some thought I was possessed by the Devil and could not escape even if I fled to the ends of the land.

Continue on the lane out of Chelmick for about a quarter of a mile until you go through an area of trees on either side of the lane as it goes into a left bend and here look carefully on the right for a stile under a holly tree. Cross onto a fairly steep downward course keeping to the right boundary of a field. There are some fishing pools below in the valley. You reach a gate at the bottom; go through it and turn right onto a metalled lane. Now your map, if you have got one that is, might show the official right of way as going through a gate 15 yards on your right, across a small field, out through another gate and up a bank onto a stony track. However the first gate might well be chained up and, in any event, it seems much more logical to continue along the tarmac for 50 yards and turn right directly onto the track.

You go past a cottage, through yet another gate and walk across the front of a stone built house and onto a narrow path the other side between trees. You shortly pass a very isolated property and stay ahead on the obvious path which will look very pretty in spring when the bluebells, primroses and a host of other flowers are in bloom. The path can get very churned up by horses, so proceed with care. You are soon confronted by two gates side by side – take the left option to continue along the path, passing a stables complex before finally going through a further gate and turning left on a stony drive to meet a lane.

Cross the lane and go over the stile directly opposite into a meadow, then cross another stile about 70 yards ahead adjacent to a cottage. In the next field keep to right boundary and cross a further stile about 100 yards ahead and stay ahead towards a tree lined brook. Oh dear! This is not the right way at all. I'm afraid you will have to reverse your steps all the way back to the lane to stay on the Jack Mytton Way, ha ha… Well, come on, get on with it!

Alternatively, you could just stay on this path unless absolutely determined to follow the 'official' JM path to the letter. It is a short cut and avoids another section of your tarmac. So, cross the brook via a footbridge then go directly ahead cutting off the little bit of the bottom corner of a field to meet a post & wire fence on the right – turn left in front of it and follow it up the field to the end where you cross a stile onto a lane. If you encounter any boggy ground on the way, too bad.

Turn left on the lane and stay on it as it drops down through the pretty village of Ticklerton, where you take the left turn towards Wall and Much Wenlock. Ignore a turning right after 150 yards then one on the left shortly afterwards and continue on the lane for another half mile or so.

Most victims of my practical joking were compensated either with drink or money, and that included Mr Owen. One day I laid the wire of a spring-gun in the path I knew he took on his way to church. When he let off the trap I accused him of shooting at pheasants on a Sunday. He was so overcome that he would not face his congregation until a suitable amount of liquor had been poured down his throat! My reaction to bores was even more disconcerting. I had the misfortune to be with one in a coffee shop once and dropped a burning coal into his pocket. It soon shut him up when he had to flee outside and jump into the nearest horse trough.

Racing became my passion in the early 1820s when I had thirteen horses in training. But I attracted trouble like a magnet. Some just came to a race meeting in the hope of seeing me in a brawl and often were not disappointed. That's he! That's Mytton! I heard them cry, then proceeded to stir up a fight to see if I would join in. My reputation was now at a very low point.

George III, the mad King died, George IV (a man after my own heart!) was crowned, Bonaparte died, I lost the Albrighton Hunt, lost money on gambling and stayed drunk. Mr Owen urged me to re-marry and it so happened that Apperley had taken a house at Brewood in the neighbourhood of the Giffards of Chillington, a large sporting family of some distinction. Invitations were forthcoming and, to cut a long story short, I became captivated by the seventeen year old Caroline Giffard and married her on 29th October, 1821, much to the grave apprehension of her family.

For a while things were better. I kept away from drink and hounds and she was neither clinging nor given to silly chatter. She had good humour and even took my practical jokes in good spirit. By December she was pregnant and life at Halston was for once stable and relaxed. Barbara Augusta was born the following August and, again I was devastated that I did not have a son. Happily this did not last and soon Caroline was expecting again. Although still inclined towards pranks and losing money on horse dealing, I was it seems sufficiently reformed to be appointed High Sheriff of Shropshire in early 1823. I became a hero with the residents of Oswestry for breaking up an ugly march by striking miners and Caroline was immensely proud of me. In November she produced a son, John Fox Fitzgiffard, and Halston had not seen celebrations like it since I became of age.

After going through a right hand bend turn off left across a pull-in to enter a bridleway (not waymarked). Now this often gets very churned up and, if it is, you can divert through a break in the hedgeline left into the field and walk parallel to the track (sissies). You eventually exit onto a lane after about half a mile.

I suppose it was inevitable that I would become bored with this domestic bliss. The bottle began to once more assume its prominent role in my life and tavern girls started to catch my eye. Caroline pretended not to notice these things or my increasingly silly exploits. Like the mock hunt with all the servants mounted upon ponies, donkeys and mules or betting on a race between carthorses. Staid, respectable county life did not, I decided, at all suit my pleasure and I sank again into a drunken, loutish and ever more eccentric existence, riding around on my bear and causing mayhem with my inebriated cronies. Caroline tried desperately to bring me back to some normality but we became more and more estranged.

My term as High Sheriff ended and I shrugged off the last remnants of respectability. I left Caroline at home and went in search of excitement elsewhere, causing trouble wherever I went. Bills for damage were frequent – well I suppose if you let a fox loose in an hotel with a brace of dogs to chase it, for example, the fixtures and fittings are unlikely to survive unscathed. A second son arrived in early 1825 but this only increased my distaste for the nursery and increased my promiscuity. I was cruel and heartless, I admit it now to my bitter regret, all the more so because my wife was a loyal and forgiving woman.

Turn left then immediately right along a track signed 'Mount Flirt' and 'Belvidere'. Where it bears right cross a stile alongside a gate into a field and continue the line forward to the left of the boundary hedge. After about 80 yards you go through a gate into the adjacent field to continue the line but now to the right of the boundary fence. We now have a closer view of Hope Bowdler and Helmuth Hills. At the end of the field in the tree line there are two stiles – take the one ahead into the trees on a steep downward track, so care is required if you want to finish the walk in a vertical position. Where the path levels out at the bottom you will find a stile to cross followed quickly by a footbridge. Once in the field on the other side climb upwards to a gate in the right corner. This leads you into another field with the church of Hope Bowdler over to the half left. Continue ahead to a stile which in turn leads you onto a track between fence and hedge. After a short distance turn right through a timber gate then immediately left in front of some cottages and to the right of the church. Pause awhile here if you wish and consider the next stage of my miserable existence.

The arrival of another son temporarily restored my sense of responsibility but this did not last and I spiralled ever closer towards the abyss, with long drinking bouts in dubious company, black moods and heavy gambling losses. The financial situation became precarious indeed. Stories of my many liaisons (usually ending with a cash transaction) and outrageous exploits in and around Shrewsbury heaped embarrassment and shame upon my family and the Giffards. A fourth son was born in April 1827 but I was hardly aware of his existence. If asked how many children I had I would be hard put to answer the question correctly.

George IV died grotesquely with dropsy and was succeeded by William IV but I was totally unaware of it or, indeed, of anything else going on in the world. Alcoholism had tightened its grip and this time it would not let go. I was filled with morbid despair and delusion, imagining that everyone was against me and plotting attempts on my life. Sometimes I would leap upon my horse and ride away in terror or attack innocent people for no reason. The door of Chillington was closed to me but still Caroline remained loyal – until the day I attacked her in a fit of drunken rage. Mercifully she was not harmed but fled to Chillington with our children for safety. A few weeks later a Bill of Complaints was presented in the names of Caroline and the children which stated, amongst other things, that 'John Mytton wholly gave himself up to a life of the greatest profligacy'. The complaint was granted and Caroline remained at Chillington under her brother's protection.

At about this time the Tory Government fell and a General Election ensued. In a half-crazed state I offered myself as a candidate and arrived in Shrewsbury looking for support. Instead, I was greeted with derision and suffered defeat at the hands of Sir Rowland Hill. In fact I came bottom of the poll and retired ignominiously to Birmingham, not even daring to stay in the Shire where I had become cold-shouldered. I drifted to London and took rooms at Pulteney's Hotel, which I had known in better days. Now the bailiffs were in pursuit of me and I stupidly imagined that Caroline would look after me and comfort me as she had in the past. When I arrived at Chillington I was set upon by servants and led away with bound wrists. I was never to see my wife again.

Proceed through the village and exit onto the B4371. Turn right on the road and, after about 120 yards, cross carefully and branch off left along a broad waymarked path between properties. After a short distance bear left following the sign to Church Stretton and Gaerstone over a stile onto a narrow path. Shortly cross another stile and another to follow an attractive course alongside a brook. Cross a further stile and continue forward around the base of Gaer rock and cross the next stile to continue around the base to cross yet another stile before continuing onwards to the right of a pair of solitary ash trees. Cross another stile which directs you diagonally left across a field to the right of an electricity pole to a stile in the hedge on the opposite side. Cross this onto the B4371 again.

Turn right then immediately right again to commence the climb up to Gaer Rock. Only joking! There is a path up if you have the energy but I would make back to town now and find a good tavern. Continue on the road for about 120 yards until it goes into a left bend where we depart from it to the right along a waymarked track and over a stile into a field to the right of a post and wire fence. It is now that the Long Mynd comes into view. At the end of the field cross another stile and proceed in the next field for a short distance until the fence on your left turns left downhill. Here you continue the line forward diagonally down and across a large field aiming for a house in view close to the bottom right corner. Beyond the house in the field corner is a stile to cross and turn left onto a narrow tarmac lane. After about 120 yards climb some steps and cross a waymarked stile on the right into a field and, at the end, cross a track with stiles on each side into the adjacent field which you traverse directly down to the A49.

Cross the main road carefully as those mobile tins come whizzing along, and go over a stile then immediately through a gate on the right into a field following a post & wire fence on your left heading towards town. You need to cross a stile and railway line very carefully (glad this wasn't here in my day too) then another stile on the other side and follow a public footpath sign through the grounds of a residential home to exit via a gate. Cross the road onto a waymarked path alongside a brook. Once out into playing fields turn left to cross a footbridge into the adjacent section of playing field to the rear of houses and walk along the bottom edge At the end of the playing field go through onto a path between gardens and out onto a street. Turn left and immediately right and follow this into the main street and back to the start.

I returned to London and placed myself in the hands of my solicitors. Shortly thereafter the effects at Halston were sold to pay my debts and a petition for bankruptcy filed. In the depths of despair I fled to France to see my old friend Apperley and, deranged with drink, started to brag about the new fortune I was going to make; how I would start a new stable, refurnish Halston and get my wife back! 'I'll have my wife back again, by God! Look at these marks, they handcuffed me, but so help me God, I'll have her yet!' Apperley tried to help but to no avail. Then I met with a terrible accident.

I returned to my room one night with a companion (I won't say friend, he was a rogue) both drunk as lords. I began to hiccup and tried to frighten it away by setting fire to my shirt tails! Instantly I was a mass of flames – the other man threw me to the floor and tore away the burning material, removing most of my skin as well. The pain was terrible and only anaesthetized by copious quantities of brandy. My friends feared for my sanity and Apperley said to me 'Mytton, your doctors assure me that you will be a corpse in three days unless you give up drinking brandy' 'So much the better' I said, 'I wish to die'.

By some miracle I recovered and returned to London in June 1832 promising to behave myself. Needless to say, I was still plagued with debt and pursued ruthlessly by I don't know how many bailiffs. Why I went back to Halston with some notion of, yet again, standing for Parliament can only be put down to insanity. The house was empty and stripped of all its old homely things though I remained hidden there for several months until my inevitable arrest. Friends, who were now few in number, offered to lend me money, but there were strings attached and I refused. My committal to the King's Bench Prison followed – a pathetic, drink sodden, wreck.

The sale of Halston timber paid off my debts and I was released onto the streets of London. I started losing at gambling once more and soon the Bailiffs were on my heels again. I fled to France with a lover I had taken called Susan and ended up in Lille. We quarrelled and she left me, at which point I drank heavily and got into a fight. I arrived at Apperley's house without a shirt and covered with blood. My mother came to bring me back to England and I said goodbye to my old friend who had borne my shortcomings with great fortitude – I would never see him again.

I was now 37 years of age. Halston's glory days were gone and its melancholy silence got on my nerves. I slipped back into my old ways – drunk and in debt. In January 1834 I was arrested again for debts and sent back to Kings Bench Prison where I continued to drink heavily to ease the pain of an ulcerated leg. My God! I had plumbed the depths of the darkest imaginable despair. Who would now recognize this bloated, decrepit, disease ridden dreg of humanity who was once the toast of Shropshire?

Three weeks later I had a stroke which paralysed my legs and by March 29th I was delirious. My mother came to stay at the prison and held me in her arms but, that evening, I suffered another stroke and was dead before she could lay me back on the pillow.

Despite the hurt I had caused so many in my life I was utterly amazed at the regard in which I was apparently held. After *removal of my body to Shrewsbury a splendid funeral cortege conveyed it to the vault at Halston. There were a score of mourning carriages, a hundred riders in procession and nearly three thousand people lining the route [2]. Tears were running down their faces – the Squire had come home and old grudges were forgiven.*

Notes:

1. The Jack Mytton Way is a 70 mile path from the Severn Valley to Llanfair Waterdine on the Welsh Border.

2. On the day of his funeral all shops were closed and bells tolled in Ellesmere and Whittington. It is said that the burial party halted for the night at a coaching inn now known as the Mytton and Mermaid at Atcham where a rumour persists to this day that his ghost roams the corridors of the hotel where he had once spent time in the company of his friends before taking the path to oblivion.

Bibliography:

The Life and Times of Squire John Mytton of Halston, Holdsworth, Jean, 1972
Tales of Old Shropshire, Lawrence-Smith, Kathleen, 1991

14

Ippikin

Sometime in the twelfth century

Maps: Landranger 138; Explorer 217

Start/Park: You can start from the National Trust car park on the B4371 at Presthope, about 2½ miles south-west of Much Wenlock and a mile past the aggregate quarry at Presthope.(GR 584976). However, my preferred starting point is the village of Hughley because the route from there fits better with the story and you can get a drink/meal towards the end of the walk at the Wenlock Edge Inn. To get to Hughley, take the right turn (travelling from the Much Wenlock direction) immediately after the car park referred to and follow it for a little over a mile. GR565979. Car parking spaces in the village are restricted so please park sensibly – there are a couple of spaces outside the church which could be used when a service is not in progress or due and there is some limited verge parking. If you continue past the church and out of the other side of the village there is plenty of verge parking if the ground is not too soft.

Walk distance/Terrain: 7 miles, although it may feel longer. There is some stiff climbing up Wenlock Edge so please DO NOT attempt the walk unless you are reasonably fit.

Refreshments: The Wenlock Edge Inn (excellent)

Associated place of interest:

Wenlock Edge – Formed about 420 million years ago and running in an unbroken line for 15 miles. A large part of it is owned by the National Trust and there is much to see and do there. A visit to the Tourist Office in Much Wenlock would be worthwhile.

I don't suppose many of you have heard of me. Ippikin – who was Ippikin? If you had lived round here in the twelfth century you would have heard of me alright. Suffered at my hands I shouldn't wonder. Now I'm condemned to folklore... or am I? Perhaps you might find out later, but have a care!

From the church go towards Wenlock Edge and take the first turning left along a no through road after about 80 yards. You shortly pass Town Farm. Stay on it as the surface deteriorates into a track and

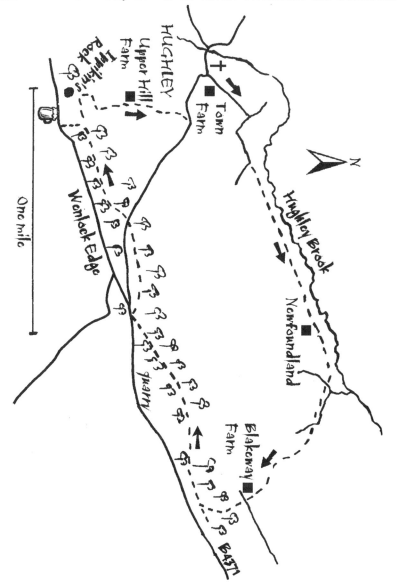

twists right then left. Go over a cattle barrier after which the track continues along the left edge of a large field. Ignore a stile on the left and a little further on cross another cattle barrier. On reaching a third cattle barrier there is a choice of ways.

If you haven't heard of me you will have heard about Robin Hood. Well, I did the same as him – robbed travellers. At around the same time in history too. Except that I was bigger than him, much uglier, fiercer and never gave to the poor. Pah, they didn't deserve it anyway and never did anything for the likes of me. Me, a knight no less, having come back from serving the King at the Crusades only to find that my services were no longer needed. That's gratitude for you. Well, I chose to make my living in another way and to hell with 'em, I'll rob 'em instead and kill 'em if they resist.

Go left which is sort of straight ahead keeping to the right of a wooded area at first. Where the hedge line veers off left after about 50 yards continue ahead to join another hedge line on the right which runs along the rear of the garden to Newfoundland Farmhouse. Gardens! What sissy things they are, and tiny too. I would have felt hemmed in if that's all I had to wander around in. My domain was the entire area you can see about and no one stopped me from going anywhere I liked. If this is how you have to live you can keep it.

At the end of the garden continue ahead in a field and shortly meet another tree boundary on the left. Go forward on the obvious path along the ridge of the field above the trees and as you near the end of the field you need to go right down a slope to what effectively is the bottom right corner where there is a stile and footbridge across Hughley Brook[1].Footbridge – huh, we did not need such aids. What's wrong with just splashing across? Frightened to get your feet wet?

You come out into a field and stay ahead until you reach another section of brook where you turn right along a narrow path through some trees with the brook below on your left. You cross a little stream where there is a marker post and you stay ahead to the right of a fence and trees. You next arrive at a crossing boundary formed by parallel lines of small trees and you turn right here alongside them. At the top you go through a wicket gate which leads you out into another largish field.

You continue the gradual climb to the left of a boundary hedge heading right for Wenlock Edge. At the top you come out at Blakeway Farm and cross a track directly through a timber gate, again in an upward direction. This brings you out in a clearing where you bear round to the right to continue upwards.

After what I expect will have been an exhausting climb for you, you reach the top and a broad crossing track. Turn right. Ignore a left turn uphill after a short distance. After a while you can (optionally) divert off left up some steps to Major's Leap – a stiff half-mile climb to reach it[2]. Eventually you come to a marked fork and keep left uphill and you arrive at a parking place for horseless wagons.

Now me and my bandits terrorized the locality and became feared by everyone. I lived in a cave beneath the Edge but no one dared attack it even though it was full of booty and treasure. People with things of value had to hire armed men to protect it! Most people who were unfortunate enough to be waylaid handed over their jewellery and money without so much as a whimper 'cause they knew our reputation for slitting the throats of any who resisted. Oh yes, many a person has seen his last moment in the shadow of Wenlock Edge, particularly those from other parts who were not well informed.

All sorts of rumours sprang up about who I was – my favourite was that I was an ancient magician who had found the secret of renewing life every 70 years. Another was that I had a very, very long chin – true up to a point (ho, ho – joke!). My nefarious (a big word for a twelfth century robber, but, as I told you I was formerly a knight with a good upbringing) exploits could not last forever and eventually I got my comeuppance. One night during a violent storm lightning struck a huge rock overhanging my cave and over it toppled to come crashing down across the entrance. My fellow robbers and I were trapped inside.

Don't actually go into the parking place but 20 yards before it turn right along a green path signed Easthope Wood. Descend some steps which end as you continue narrowly downwards along a path that can get overgrown and a little boggy and you reach a fork where you go left up steps still following the green sign to Easthope Wood. Keep going to come out onto a lane.

Turn right then immediately left to follow the sign to Easthope Wood. Again this is a steep path (Jack Mytton Way[3]). Go over a crossing path to continue upwards. This crossing path is the route of an old railway line[4] and here there is a sign pointing the way to Ippikin's Rock. Keep right at a junction and shortly after ignore a path uphill to the left. The ground can get very muddy around here. It was muddy everywhere in my day with constant churning up by horses and carts.

You pass under a large outcrop of rock on your left which is visible through the trees and shortly after this ignore another path uphill to the left. You will come to a further left path uphill which is waymarked Ippikin's Rock and you take this and climb up to go over a stile and on to the rock. See, I was not so obscure, they know which is my rock from where I had a superb view of everything and everyone passing beneath and they have named a footpath after me! Over to the left you can see The Lawley and

Caer Caradoc with the Long Mynd behind it and the village of Hughley to the half right where the walk started.

Now, are you feeling brave? Are the legends true and does my ghost still roam the Edge threatening doubters and the unwary? It is said that if you are foolish enough to challenge the ghost of old Ippikin on this rock with the words 'Ippikin, Ippikin keep away with your long chin' I will appear with a large gold chain around my neck and, with one blow, sweep you over the precipice. Dare you take the risk – you have been warned!

If you survive the rock and fancy some refreshment go out from the back of it and out across fields passing through three gates to reach, via the wagon park, the Wenlock Edge Inn. A splendid hostelry serving meals and snacks. I wish it had been there in my day; mind you I would have robbed all the customers!

Otherwise, or on leaving the Inn re-trace your steps back to the path below the rock and turn left. After about 250 yards look very carefully for a stile on the right in the trees. Cross and turn right across the top of a sloping field with Upper Hill Farm in view ahead. The correct path is probably about half way down the slope but it is not critical although the ground is fairly rough and you ninnies should pick whichever route is easiest.

When you are almost level with the farm outbuildings you reach a point where there is an ash tree in the centre of the field and here bear left down the field to a stile visible in the bottom boundary. Cross this and the next field to another stile in front of the end barn. Turn right towards the farm then left with a waymark placed on the end of the first barn, down a concrete ramp and follow that right around the rear of the next barn. At the end you can see a stile taking you into a large field where you need to bear half left towards the village of Hughley you can see ahead, aiming for four trees in the far boundary with a farm someway to the rear. If you are lucky the farmer will have marked the way across.

There is a gate in the hedge and once in the next field walk by the right boundary heading towards some farm buildings. Just to the right of them you will find a waymarked stile by a gate. Cross onto a shaled track in front of the farmhouse after which it loops left to join a lane. Turn left on the lane back into Hughley [5].

If you are reading this you must have 'chickened out' of my challenge or perhaps I am just getting a little tired of throwing people off the edge. Anyway, I hope you enjoyed the walk and will no doubt go home now to ease your aching feet and legs.

Notes:

1. At the time of research the footbridge had been torn from its mountings by floods but it was still possible to get across with a little agility. Hopefully it has now been repaired.

2. Majors Leap so named after Major Smallman of Wilderhope Manor nearby who was a royalist in the Civil War. He was trapped in the Hall by Roundheads but escaped with his enemies in hot pursuit. When cornered at a sheer drop on Wenlock Edge he jumped off with his horse. The horse died but the Major survived.

3. Jack Mytton – see walk Nos 12 and 13.

4. A former branch of the GWR running between Wellington and Craven Arms.

5. Hughley Steeple is famous for a steeple that was never here, as set down in verse by A.E.Houseman in *A Shropshire Lad* 'The vane of Hughley steeple veers bright....' The bell tower dates from 1701 and the clock was a gift from a proud owner after his horse won the Derby in 1892. It is well known for being inaccurate!

15

Wild Humphrey Kynaston

1470? – 1534

Maps: Landranger 126; Explorer 240
Start: At Nesscliffe on the A5 between Shrewsbury and Oswestry. Turn right opposite the Old Three Pigeons Pub along a lane and you will find a car park after about half a mile on the right. GR 386199
Walk Distance: about 5 miles. It involves a steep descent on steps down to Kynaston's Cave so should not be undertaken by anyone who is in any way infirm.
Terrain: A mixture of easy well used paths and some climbing. See note above. Excellent views.
Refreshments: The Old Three Pigeons at Nesscliffe (highly recommended).
Associated places of interest:
1. Myddle Castle is situated at Castle Farm behind the church and is accessible by public paths, although the ruin itself is fenced off.
2. Montford Bridge – 5 miles to the south-east of Nesscliffe, also on the A5.

SIR Humphrey Kynaston if you don't mind! A real Elizabethan Robin Hood, make no mistake and one of the best highwaymen that ever stalked the land. Born a gent but couldn't hack it (as you would say), died an outlaw but was never captured. Mark you, they tried often enough but I was just a bit too quick for 'em, and a mite cleverer though I say so myself. I will tell you more of this anon.

Continue along the lane (don't follow a marker into the wood) pass a farm and turn right. The lane climbs and at the top turn left at a marker along broad track in a wood.

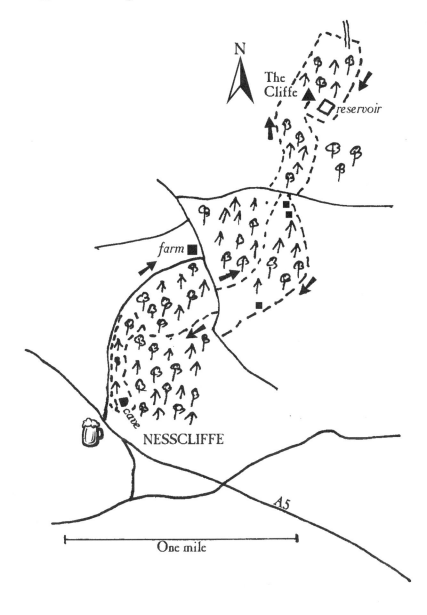

If you go to the village of Myddle, some seven miles to the north-east of here, you will see what remains of my birthright – a single crumbling tower of the once sumptuous castle I inherited from my father Sir Roger Kynaston. Legend has it, quite rightly, that I led a dissolute and riotous life which put me in great debt. This was how I came to be known as 'Wild' Humphrey Kynaston but I don't think it would be proper for me to embarrass you educated folks with a detailed account of my antics. Suffice it to say that I squandered my money till there was none left and neglected the property in the most irresponsible manner.

Now most historical journals of your day will say that I was outlawed in 1491 for my debts. This is not strictly true – there was the small matter of the murder of one John Heughes at Stretton in that particular year for which I, and two others, were indicted for the said heinous crime. True, I struck the first blow with a lance but then Thomas, my half-brother, pitched in with a sword stroke and then Robert Hopton finished it off with a pike. They said that I struck what was the fatal blow and thus the onus of murder rested upon me, whereupon I immediately decamped, remained in concealment and was in consequence outlawed.

You pass a car park and continue in beautiful mixed woodland. Ignore a marker right and stay on the 'red' path. This opens out to the right with views over north Shropshire. Pass a sandstone cottage and descend to another lane. Turn left then immediately right up a marked track. After 70 yards bear right at a marker post and on meeting a broader track turn sharp left uphill on sandstone bedrock. Keep ahead at a crossing track but after another 25 yards go left at a fork on a path around the base of 'The Cliffe'. Keep going on this path for a time until reaching a white cottage and stables.

Reports will show that no less than three dozen persons of all ranks of society did after the murder 'feloniously receive, comfort, feed, lodge and maintain' me and my co-accused. Among these was my father, Sir Roger, two others styled gentlemen, one tailor, one baker, one sherman, two drapers, three chapmen, one bower, one mercer, one yeoman, one drover and twenty husbandmen. That such men should have been capable of assisting and sheltering men known to have been guilty of murderous outrages was beyond belief, it was said.

Thus I was an outcast and made my way to Nesscliffe where I could take refuge from the Sheriff's men in the woods there. I soon found shelter in a cave in the sandstone rock and this was to be my home for many years. You can visit it today and will indeed do so a little later.

Turn right alongside the cottage up a track. On meeting the cottage driveway, cross it and follow the marker to climb the path through a wood. Ignore crossing paths until reaching a fenced reservoir. With the reservoir on your right, at the corner turn right to reach a viewpoint with a picnic table and information board. Turn right, again still with the fence on the right, to arrive at the trig point and second view point with a bench. This was my domain, or at least the immediately surrounding countryside was. A good vantage point for seeing who was about, what? You also get good

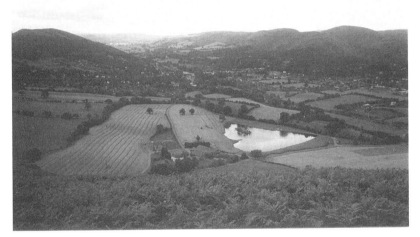

View from The Cliffe

Extract from information panel showing my leap over the River Severn

views of the Breiddons and, right in the distance, the Welsh Hills. I would often come here to 'cleanse my soul'

Even though my name was reviled by 'respectable' people I never lost my sense of justice. I stole, yes, but only from the wealthy who travelled the high road and most of this I gave to the poor who lived in the area. In return they protected me and took food and hay for my horse. As I said, Robin Hood in another guise! The Sheriff and his men made numerous attempts to capture me but never succeeded. On one occasion I got over the River Severn by Montford Bridge towards Shrewsbury and having to reach my cave again, obviously to re-cross the bridge, the Under-Sheriff with a number of men lay in ambush. The bridge was then made of stone pillars and planks laid between the pillars. They took up several of the planks and left such a chasm as they thought no horse could leap over. When, on my return, I was about to enter the bridge they made an attempt to seize me but, seeing their intention, I put spurs to my horse and with desperate resolution leapt over the space and escaped. The measure of this leap was afterwards marked out on the Knockin Heath with an H and K cut in the ground to show the length of it, known as 'Kynaston's Leap'. A full 40 feet it was. All were astounded and the letters were, for a long time, cleaned and repaired each year but you won't find them now as they are completely overgrown.

I remember well the day I rode into the yard of Aston Hall and called for a drink. The servant brought me a silver tankard of ale for which I thanked him, but did not dismount. As I was drinking the ale they closed the gates of the courtyard so as to trap me inside. Obviously the servant had recognized me as the infamous outlaw and raised the alarm. Anyway, I determined to finish my ale, slipped the tankard into my pocket and set my horse at a group of the men. The horse sprang forward, cleared both men and the gates and I was free. Needless to say I was a little more careful in future!

As I said, I retained a sense of justice and much of what I stole I gave to the poor who lived nearby. It was said that if ever I met two carts out on the road and one had three horses pulling it and the other only one, I would take the lead horse of the three and give it to the other cart just to even things up! Well maybe, but to most people I was a lawless criminal and I did scare the daylights out o' some of 'em I must say. Serves 'em right though – it was them or toffs like them who made me an outlaw in the first place.

When ready, return to the information board and turn left downhill, then right at a junction on a sandy track. At another junction turn right (not sharp right along the red path) down to meet a lane. Turn right on the lane but after 100 yards turn left by a telephone box (hey, what fun I could have had in my day with your phones – can you imagine how I would have led the sheriff's men a merry chase and organized my mates to let me know whenever danger threatened!) along a broad track. You pass some smart houses after which the track turns to sand/grass. Ignore a marker to the right and keep to the edge of the wood until

The steps to Kynaston's Cave

coming out onto a driveway by a sandstone cottage. Ignore the marker right and proceed to meet lane and turn right.

Before reaching the top of the hill turn off left down marked track by a cottage signed Kynaston's Cave, on the orange path. After a few yards go ahead at a marker still on the orange path, signed viewpoint – DO NOT go left on the path signed Kynaston's Cave this time. An Iron Age fort is up on the right hidden in the trees which was not there then. Later it was used by the Romans then by Cromwell's soldiers as a look-out post. I also used it as a look-out post but history does not record that!

Ignore a marker right, in fact departing now from the orange path, and shortly go right then right again at a picnic spot to another viewpoint. Bit of a climb this but there are splendid views across North Shropshire, the Welsh Hills, and Rodney's Pillar to the left[1]. From here backtrack to the picnic area and you go across it to enter on an opposite path through rhododendrons. Keep going for some time until you reach steps down to Kynaston's Cave. Now, the point of access may not be all that obvious – you will come to a small (and I mean small) clearing and the steps are down to the right partially obscured by vegetation.

Kynaston's Cave

It's a steep descent so take great care even though there is a fence to prevent a fearsome drop into an old sandstone quarry. As you negotiate the steps keep an eye out for names and initials carved in the face of the sandstone cliff. Many of them are dated 1866 and I can only assume from their inaccessible position that they were carved by the quarry workers as the face was cut away.

When you reach the bottom stay on the obvious path until you arrive at the cave. Please, go and have a look at it. Your people have kindly provided a staircase for this purpose although you will readily appreciate that I had to use the sandstone flight of steps cut in the rock! No safety barriers in those days. There are two small rooms divided by a pillar of rock. Not much I know, in your terms, but it served me well for many a year and I made it quite comfortable. The villagers kept me and my horse supplied with food hidden in a trough at the base of the cave. You can still see this if you look closely. You may also find the initials 'HK' carved into the rock and the date 1564. As I actually died in 1534 this must have been added later, or I was drunk at the time!

Now, you remember me referring to my horse? Now we are here I can tell you that he was no ordinary horse! His name was Beelzebub (the local villagers named him thus) and by day he grazed in the meadows nearby but when I whistled he would come to me at a gallop. At night he climbed the cave steps to his stable in the outer room. He did get a bit smelly but, then, so did I. My favourite trick to elude any who would aspire to capturing me was to put the horse's shoes on backwards so that the followers would be led in the opposite direction! Clever eh?

Now I know that I became a legend and so did my horse by way of his jumping feats but sometimes, indeed frequently, legend does tend to exaggerate the truth, if there is any of that at all. The story got handed down and got mightily distorted in the process, that on one occasion when I was trying to outwit the sheriff, my horse jumped from the top of Nesscliffe and landed at Ellesmere – nine miles away! Some said I had the Devil's help to do it, others that my horse was the Devil himself. Pah!

When finished take the marked route opposite down to meet a broad track and turn right. Swing left at marker down to meet lane. The Old Three Pigeons pub is opposite (which I used to frequent, though it looked a little different then). I strongly recommend a visit as there are some artifacts in there relating to my life, including my cave seat which is carved into the fireplace. There is also an account of my misdeeds hanging nearby [2].

On departure go back up to the marker last referred to but here turn off left up some steps and walk along a rough path at the base of the tree line. You eventually enter the trees; ignore a marker on the left but, at the second a short distance further on you will find yourself back at the starting point.

As I said earlier I died in 1534, or history has recorded it thus. Where history disagrees is regarding the later phase of my life and place of death. Some say that I was pardoned for my crimes in 1516 and thereafter went to live and die peacefully in a modest property in Welshpool. Other accounts, including the one in the Old Three Pigeons, say that I was never captured and died in my cave at the age of 56. So, which version would you like to believe – the boring one or the romantic one? Unfortunately for you romantics I have to tell you that I was pardoned and the document to prove it has been preserved by my family, which suggests that the Old Three Pigeons have got it wrong or are romanticizing the story for the benefit of visitors. Or have they? Perhaps there is truth in both versions.

Notes:

1. Admiral Lord Rodney. The pillar was erected on the summit of Breiddon Hill in 1781 to commemorate his naval victories against the French.

2. There would appear to be some confusion over Kynaston's age as well as how he spent his later years. The account in the Old Three pigeons states his date of birth to be 1478 which, if correct, would have made him 13 when indicted for murder. Other accounts give his date of birth as 1470 which seems more plausible.

Bibliography:

Tales of Old Shropshire, Kathleen Lawrence-Smith, 1991

Various extracts from records in Shrewsbury Library.

Also by Roger Seedhouse…

> *Visit* www.bestwalks.com *for more information.*

Walks to Wet your Whistle

The walks in this book cover some of the most beautiful countryside in Shropshire and along its Staffordshire borders. From quiet rural backwaters to scenic hill country there is plenty to suit every taste. The book will appeal both to more experienced walkers and, by the introduction of shorter alternatives, to casual walkers or those wishing to vary the length of their walk as mood or time constraints dictate.

The eighteen main walks of between 7 and 11½ miles are arranged with a pub break conveniently located as near to half-way as possible. Short alternatives start and finish at the pub and range in distance between 2¾ and 5¼ miles.

ISBN 1 869922 41 7. 112 pages. £6.95. 17 photographs. 18 maps.

More Walks to Wet your Whistle

Roger Seedhouse here presents a second collection of eighteen walks covering some more of the most beautiful countryside in Shropshire and along its border with Staffordshire. As in the first book there is plenty to suit every taste with main walks of between 6 and 10½ miles having a pub break at about the half-way stage and shorter alternatives of between 2½ and 5 miles starting and finishing at the pub.

ISBN 1 869922 36 0. £6.95. 112 pages. 24 photographs. 18 maps.

Walks through History in the Heart of England

The twenty-four walks in this book offer the enquiring walker many intriguing glimpses of a bygone age – with iron-age forts, battle sites, medieval castles and even a second world war camp. Most are based on English Heritage sites, but others are included because of their particular interest.

Walking distances vary from 3 miles to 13½ miles (although this longer one can be divided up to create two separate walks). All of them start at, or pass through, places of historical interest that will add greatly to your appreciation of a day out in beautiful walking country. Most have good pubs *en route*.

ISBN 1 869922 41 7. £8.95. 160 pages. 38 photographs. 24 maps.

Available from booksellers or, if in difficulty, direct from the publishers. Please send your remittance, including the following amounts for postage and packing: Order value up to £10.00 add £1.00; over £10.00 and up to £20.00 add £2.00; over £20.00 add £2.50.

Meridian Books 40 Hadzor Road Oldbury West Midlands B68 9LA

Please send for our complete catalogue

Also from Meridian…

Country Walks in Warwickshire and Worcestershire

by Des Wright

Twenty circular walks in two fine counties from a popular author whose love of the countryside is abundantly evident in this book. The walks explore some of the counties' most attractive areas, with easy walking, mostly on the flat and with few climbs. Distances range from 2½ to 8½ miles although some can be combined to give longer walks.

ISBN 1 869922 33 6. £5.95. 96 pages. 16 photographs. 21 maps.

More Country Walks in Warwickshire and Worcestershire

by Des Wright

A second collection of circular walks. As in the first collection the walking is not difficult with few climbs. Distances range from 4½ to 11½ miles, with most walks having a shorter option of between 1½ and 8 miles. All are readily accessible by car and by public transport.

ISBN 1 869922 37 9. £5.95. 112 pages. 22 photographs. 20 maps.

Walks in South Warwickshire

From Shakespeare Country to the Cotswolds

by John W Parnham and Barry R Wills

This collection of circular walks will take you along ancient trackways and paths, past standing stones, earthworks, country estates and grand houses. In the Arden countryside as well as finding connections to William Shakespeare you will discover hidden valleys and distinct wooded hilltops that offer wonderful views. Further south the walks will take you through delightful villages and into remote areas in the Cotswold Hills that rival in many ways the better known parts of this beautiful region.

ISBN 1 869922 38 7. Price £6.95. 112 pages. 36 sketches. 18 maps.

Walks Around the Malverns

by Roy Woodcock

The Malvern Hills and their surroundings provide magnificent opportunities for rambling, and in this book of twenty walks Roy Woodcock explores many of their superb features. Distances range from two miles to eight miles, plus a leg stretcher of between ten and sixteen miles (depending on the starting point) that takes in the full length of the ridge and ascends all the Malvern peaks.

ISBN 1 869922 32 8. £6.95. 112 pages. 32 illustrations. 20 maps.

The Navigation Way
A Hundred Mile Towpath Walk
by Peter Groves and Trevor Antill

Starting from the centre of Birmingham and encompassing fourteen West Midlands canals the Navigation Way follows a meandering course through varied urban areas and delightful countryside until terminating at Chasewater. Now again revised to cover the many changes and improvements that have been made to the towpaths its twelve sections provide a series of walks ranging from 5¼ to 11 miles. The book also contains ten additional circular 'canal-link' walks in some of the attractive walking areas adjacent to the canals.

Third revised edition. ISBN 1 869922 35 2. £5.95. 112 pages.
34 photographs. 24 maps.

Waterside Walks in the Midlands
by Birmingham Ramblers: edited by Peter Groves

Twenty-two walks featuring brooks, streams, pools, rivers and canals. Some can be found a short distance from the centre of Britain's second city; others will take the reader further afield in the West Midlands and into the attractive counties of Warwickshire, Worcestershire, Shropshire, Staffordshire and Derbyshire.

ISBN 1 869922 09 3. £4.95. 112 pages. 28 photographs. 22 maps.

More Waterside Walks in the Midlands
by Birmingham Ramblers: edited by Peter Groves

A second collection of walks featuring brooks, streams, rivers, canals and pools – sometimes as a major aspect of a walk, sometimes as a feature to encounter as you ramble through some of the fine Midlands countryside.

ISBN 1 869922 31 X. £5.95 112 pages. 21 photographs. 18 maps.

Available from booksellers or, if in difficulty, direct from the publishers.
Please send your remittance, including the following amounts for postage and packing:
Order value up to £10.00 add £1.00;
over £10.00 and up to £20.00 add £2.00;
over £20.00 add £2.50.

Meridian Books
40 Hadzor Road Oldbury West Midlands B68 9LA
Tel: 0121-429 4397

Please send for our complete catalogue